DESIGNS FOR FENCE PALES

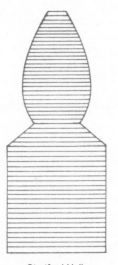

Stratford Hall
Stratford, VA

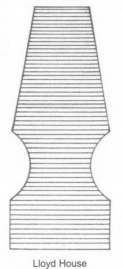

Lloyd House
Alexandria, VA

Mary Ball Washington House
Fredericksburg, VA

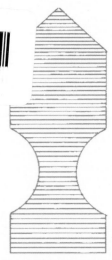

Mary Ball Washington House
Fredericksburg, VA

Cupola House
Edenton, NC

Newport, RI

Chestertown, MD

Cape May, NJ

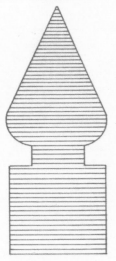

Shaker Village
Canterbury, NH

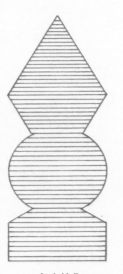

Arch Hall
Alexandria, VA

Colonial Williamsburg
Williamsburg, VA

Mount Vernon
Mount Vernon, VA

Small
Buildings
Small
Gardens

Small
Buildings
Small
Gardens

Creating Gardens
around Structures

Gordon Hayward

Gibbs Smith, Publisher
TO ENRICH AND INSPIRE HUMANKIND

Salt Lake City | Charleston | Santa Fe | Santa Barbara

First Edition
11 10 09 08 07   5 4 3 2 1

Published by
Gibbs Smith, Publisher
P.O. Box 667
Layton, Utah 84041

Orders: 1.800.835.4993
www.gibbs-smith.com

Designed by Deibra McQuiston
Printed and bound in Hong Kong

Library of Congress Cataloging-in-Publication Data
Hayward, Gordon.
  Small buildings small gardens : creating gardens
around structures / Gordon Hayward.—1st ed.
       p. cm.
  Includes bibliographical references.
  ISBN-13: 978-1-58685-705-9
  1. Gardens—Design. 2. Garden structures. I. Title. II.
Title: Creating gardens around structures.

SB473.H3895 2007
712'.6—dc22
                              2006021530

I dedicate this book to my brothers, John and Peter, and to the memory of our parents, John and Helen Hayward. As we three boys grew up on our orchard in northwestern Connecticut, we spent many happy days rambling about in the barn, shed and other outbuildings on our farm and those of our friends. I thank my brothers and our parents for all the memories gathered around the lives we shared growing up among the apple, peach and pear trees and within the old buildings we took for granted then and treasure now.

contents

Introduction

When my wife, Mary, and I started developing our garden in southern Vermont over twenty-five years ago, one of the very first gardens we made was a small herb garden that we developed in relation to an old garden shed that was on the property when we bought it. The lessons learned as we built that modest herb garden next to the little shed have held me in good stead as a garden designer over the years: gazeboes and arbors, pergolas and bridges, built structures of all kinds are hugely helpful in developing a garden design. They help you see how to develop gardens around them or to one or more sides of them. And in doing so, they help you find just the right places for plants. In fact, they anchor your thinking about where new gardens belong.

In this, my eighth book on practical garden design, I will take one more step along the road toward solid, appropriate, lasting garden design in the hopes that I can help you make those next steps in your own garden easier. My premise is this: existing or new built structures in your garden will help answer many questions you have about how to develop a design for your new or existing garden.

My feeling is that plant catalogues or garden centers that sell plants are not the sources to look to for help in developing your garden. The place to start is in its ever-expanding layout, organization and structure. The layout of your new or expanding garden gathers around the way you organize paths and places for people to sit and gather in your garden. Once you get the layout right, you have no end of appropriate places for plants.

Garden structures are in large part related to people in them—sitting in gazeboes or arbors, walking under arches and pergolas, having lunch in a summerhouse or working in a garden shed—and once you understand that garden design gathers around making places for people, you begin to find just the right places for plants that will engage those people. Just thumb through this book for a moment and you'll see what I mean.

Garden sheds and arbors, pergolas and gazeboes, fences and gates, bridges, railings and decks each provide valuable clues as to how to develop gardens around them. When you have a context for new gardens, when you begin to see that built structures in your garden provide anchors, centers and starting places for good garden design, you gain confidence as a designer of your own gardens.

After all, what you are looking for as you develop your garden are edges. Where should I put a new bed? How big should it be? What shape should it be? How does it relate to existing beds? How should I plant this new garden so it fits in with those that already exist yet adds to the overall experience of my garden? Answers to these questions can often be found in existing or built structures.

For example, take a close look at a little garden shed or a garage you already have on your property. Its doors show you where to put paths that run straight out from them, thereby breaking your big design problem down into more manageable parts. Build a simple grape arbor against that shed or garage wall and grow vines up it. Then plant a garden on either side of the arbor and put a bench under it where you can sit.

Other built structures such as fencing help you firmly establish the edges around your new garden. Each side of the fence in turn provides a background for gardens along it. Built ornaments such as obelisks and birdhouses mark centers of these new beds between shed and fence. Trellises attached to the wall of a shed provide a foothold for vines and vertical gardening.

The very nature of any garden structures already on your property, or any sheds, pergolas or gazeboes you plan to build, can help you design a garden next to or surrounding them. A practical garden shed, for example, suggests a simple fenced or hedged herb or vegetable garden, whereas a finely crafted gazebo open on four sides implies drama and views in four directions. A rustic contemplative arbor set into the corner of a woodsy area with a gate implies a haven, while a tiny garden shed with decorative details and window boxes suggests a cottage garden.

Cozy, manageable gardens snuggle up to small buildings, creating an appealing place for people. Fences, gates, bridges, trellises, obelisks and many other built structures in your garden extend the spirit of those small buildings into the landscape to help you create coherence in your garden design while also providing a lot of help in answering that ever-present question: "Where do I put this plant?"

With the growing popularity of working at home, more and more people are fitting out existing buildings, or building small houses that are weather tight, have four walls, doors and windows, and are set at a distance from the main house. Such studios, offices or summerhouses often act as anchors for gardens around them. Once you understand the power of paths to the doors and view lines through windows, you will have a starting point to develop gardens around these buildings for living:

- A small structure such as a shed in a garden suggests the dimensions, style, line and purpose of the garden adjacent to it.
- An arbor or gazebo at a distance from the house acts with the house to form bookends for a garden between them.
- Structures such as gazeboes, pergolas and summerhouses act as important destinations along a garden itinerary.
- Gazeboes, arbors and other open structures frame garden views.
- Fences, pergolas and walls provide structure, background, edges and places for people to sit, have a meal or gather.
- Gates and breaks in walls and fencing create thresholds, points of entry and transitions from one garden area to the next.
- The side of a garage, shed or barn can provide the backdrop for an arbor under which to sit within the new garden.

- Trellises and other vertical structures attached to the sides of buildings provide places for vines or espaliers.
- Bridges enable you to enter previously inaccessible areas such as wetland or the woods at the other side of a stream.

Variety is what engages visitors to a garden. If you use built structures wisely and with restraint, if you construct lasting structures in concert with a wide variety of plants for all sorts of purposes, then I think your garden will engage people. After all, as the great California garden designer Thomas Church said in the title of his most important book, "Gardens are for people."

I would like to make one last point before you move into the substance of this book, and this point has to do with how to look at photographs in a book such as this in order to gain ideas for your own garden. Don't look at the picture of an arbor or any other structure pictured in this book too literally. If you live in Michigan, you know very well that you can't grow bougainvillea on the arbor shown in figure 3.5, but you do know you can grow the *Rosa* 'New Dawn' or the orange flowering *Lonicera tellmanniana*. If you live in rustic Colorado you know this same refined white-painted arbor will not fly in cowboy country, but you have seen rustic arbors out west that would look great at your place. Think creatively. Take the spirit of and the principle behind every photograph in this book and turn those principles to your own ends. And be assured that my words will help you understand those principles in such a way that you can put them into action. If you follow this approach to creative study of the photographs herein, this book will become a valuable companion for you as you develop your garden.

Chapter 1

Arbors
Connected to
the House

W hen you marry house to garden, when the one feels related to the other, you create the feeling that you are living in a house in a garden. There is no more rewarding point to get to as a gardener and as a homeowner. No matter what size your house or garden, built structures such as arbors and fences directly connected to the house help underpin that close relationship between the two. Because arbors and fences, like decks, can literally be connected to your house, they extend the life lived in the house out into your garden.

They link one to the other in a most natural and inevitable way. And once you create that arbor off the side or end of your house or build that fence out from the corners of your house, you create a place for plants and people. Let's take a look at how people in four different states have created this union between inside and outside, between house and garden by using arbors and fencing creatively.

Small House, Small Arbor

The arbor off the gable end of Pamela and Paul Panum's guest house at their home in Eugene, Oregon, reaches only five feet into the garden from the windows and doors of the house, yet it provides that essential link between house and garden (figure 1.1). The arbor is a built wooden structure, as is the house, but the arbor is outside. It's in the garden and over the brick path; it's the coupler between house and garden. The arbor also changes the house. It provides the otherwise flat gable end with dimension, depth and detail.

Take a moment to look at all of the details of the arbor that were clearly derived from those of the house, because in many ways the house helped determine the design for this arbor, just as yours could.

- The length of the arbor is determined by the width of the four-panel windows and doors.
- The height of the arbor is raised about eighteen inches above the height of the doors to create a generous space overhead and easy egress from the adjacent room.
- The depth of the arbor is determined by the width of the brick path that passes under it.
- The color, material and style of the arbor match the trim of the house.

This arbor, in combination with the path, provides many clues for gardens associated with them. The path, which abuts the foundation of the house, acts as a step for people coming out of the guest room into the garden. It also acts as a base for two raised beds for vines that cover the arbor with foliage and flowers that fill both the area around the arbor and the interior room with fragrance and color. That solid, uniform path also provides a surface on which to place planted pots while its outer edge provides a logical place for the back edge of a bed of shrubs and perennials. The doors of the guest room provide the clue as to where a break in those shrubs and perennials should be so guests can see through those doors and walk through that gap into the larger garden beyond. The result of all these design details is that when in the guest room, people feel they are in a room in a garden. The arbor is the link, the dovetail joinery between house and garden.

This arbor also provides a space of human scale just outside this guest house. Erase that arbor from your mind and imagine how different it would be to stand a few feet out from the end of the house. As delicate as the trim work of this house is, the eighteen-foot-high gable end of the house would loom overhead; the sky would be the roof over your head. The result would be a far less appealing and comfortable space than

Figure 1.1: Attach an arbor to the side or end of a house and you do four things: enclose a walking or sitting space, provide a support for vines, make the adjacent room feel bigger, extend the house into the garden. *Garden of Pamela and Paul Panum, Eugene, Oregon.*

what you see here. Arbors create places of human scale; they provide an open airy roof overhead that lets plenty of sunlight illuminate both the area under the arbor and within the guest room.

The uprights of arbors affixed to houses also frame views in three directions. When looked at from the interior room, uprights and crosspieces frame views into the garden. When you step out of the room and stand under the arbor, uprights and crosspieces frame views to your right and left as well as straight ahead. Look closely at figure 1.1 and you'll see how the Panums took advantage of one of these frames. They placed an unpainted fence to further enclose the area at the back of their guest house, a fence that stops the eye and also acts as a backdrop for the rhododendron and adjacent gardens. Had they painted that fence white, it would have been far too insistent a color that would have made the space feel too enclosed. By leaving the wood unpainted, the fence recedes from view, thereby allowing planted pots and gardens to come forward visually. Narrow gaps between vertical boards lighten and refine the look of the fence.

Larger House, Larger Arbor

Whereas the Panums wanted a narrow arbor to add warmth and interest around doors into a guest room, Dennis Shrader and Bill Smith, who live on Long Island, New York, wanted their arbor to reach out almost twice the width of the Panums' to provide a roomy and shady sitting and entertaining area on their wooden deck (figure 1.2).

Because their arbor does not reach the outer edge of this wooden deck, it leaves some of the deck in full sun. There is an important principle at work here for you. Some people like shade, others sun; design an arbor over only the inner half or third of an existing deck, thereby leaving the outer part for sun lovers. To increase the density of shade thrown by your arbor, train a rapidly growing wisteria or some other vine appropriate to your zone to grow up the crosspieces of your arbor.

There's another simple lesson to be learned from figure 1.2. Look carefully at how Shrader and Smith enclosed the outer edges of their deck and arbor with white-painted fence, the design for which is sympathetic to the color and style of the arbor. They then used the vertical fence at the edge of their deck to support other vines that grow from garden beds below. The fencing covered in vines in turn encloses the sitting area on the deck while also acting as a backdrop for planted pots.

Now look at the far right side of figure 1.2 and you'll see yet another white-painted structure in

Figure 1.2: By attaching an arbor to their house and using the inner half of their wooden deck to support it, the owners offer guests either a shady or sunny outdoor sitting area right off their living room. *Garden of Dennis Shrader and Bill Smith, Long Island, New York.*

the garden: an arching arbor set into an ever-green hedge. By choosing a similar style and color for all three of these built structures, this one small area of their garden gains clarity on a number of levels. White underpins coherence among different garden areas and the built structures that anchor them, yet each structure has a different job:

- The arching arbor creates a feeling of entry and welcome.
- Fencing encloses the deck and provides safety at its edges.
- The arbor provides a cool, enclosed and refined place to sit during the hot summer months while at the same time reading as an extension of the house.

Fences Link House to Garden

Like decks, fences can be attached directly to the corner or corners of a house and run into the garden to enclose a garden or sitting area that can have a floor of stone, gravel, brick or other hardscaping materials. When a fence encloses a sitting area directly off the house and makes it feel private, the area feels like an extension of interior living space. Fences also provide a background for beds planted along them.

When Leslie Kammerer designed an outdoor living space for her clients in New Canaan, Connecticut (figure 1.3), she found herself having to create an intimate outdoor sitting area that could run the risk of putting her clients in a fishbowl. The second-floor windows of many neighbors' homes look down on the area, as do first-floor windows of neighbors on three sides.

The first thing Kammerer did was to enclose and define one edge of the sitting area with a five-to six-foot-high fence. Such a height would be neighborly enough to provide privacy yet not be so tall as to feel aggressive and overbearing. Wanting to refine the otherwise flat-faced fence, she added depth in two details. She insinuated a little roofed structure between panels two and three of the fence you see in figure 1.3 to break up a long expanse of faceless fence. She also used that structure to support hanging baskets. She then installed panels of trelliswork onto the fence to provide interest and detail to what could have become an otherwise bland structure.

In order to visually link vertical fencing to horizontal bluestone, Kammerer painted the wooden fence gray, a color that echoes that of the stone. She then planted light green and dark green shrubs and vines that contrast with the gray fence. The tree in the corner supports the work of the fence by providing further enclosure and privacy at heights well above that of the fence.

Figure 1.3: Fencing and trees combine to capture privacy and enclose an outdoor sitting area behind a home in a densely populated area of New Canaan, Connecticut. *Design by Leslie Kammerer.*

Fences, Gates, Arbors and Entrances

Some of the most difficult decisions you have to make as a garden designer around your own home are gathered around edges. Where does a new garden bed begin? End? How far out from the house should the bed edge be? Fencing that comes off of already-built structures such as a house, garden shed or, as you see in figure 1.4, a deck, can provide you with valuable clues as to where edges of new gardens go.

Gail and Sidney Leibovich garden near Ithaca, New York. You can see in the far left of this photograph (figure 1.4) that they have a deck, one corner of which gave rise to a fence. By attaching the fence to that corner and running it away from but parallel with the front of the deck, they were able to reach into what was featureless lawn to create a new logically placed entry garden complete with gate. So many decisions get made once you place a fence in relation to a deck or the wall of a house:

- The corner of the deck provides a logical starting place for a fence.
- The fence reaches into the adjacent area and provides new edges for gardens in front of and behind it.
- By running the stone wall and its steps parallel with the line of the fence, the logic of the placement of both is reinforced.
- The arbor and gate set into the fence lead visitors to the stone steps and into the garden.

Figure 1.4: This dramatic gate with its circular opening frames views in two directions while at the same time works with the fence to separate those same two areas. *Garden of Gail and Sidney Leibovich, Ithaca, New York.*

- Trelliswork set into the fence provides a sense of enclosure without totally shutting off gardens on either side of it.
- Trelliswork provides support for vines and vertical gardening.
- Painting all built structures white creates coherence among deck, fence, trelliswork, gate and arbor.

WHERE TO SITE AN ARBOR CONNECTED TO A HOUSE OR OTHER BUILDING

- Over the back doors of your house so as to shelter part or all of the back patio
- Over the doors of a guest room and the path leading to it
- Off the kitchen door to shelter a place for lunch or dinner
- Set into a portion of the house that is set back from the main face at the side or back of your house
- Over an existing patio or terrace connected to the house
- Off the back of a garage
- Off the side or gable end of a barn or garden shed

Chapter 2

Decks

ecks are particularly American. You may well already have one. Being made most often of wood and attached to the back of the house, they extend the floor of your house to the lawn or garden and in doing so make an outdoor place for people that is attached to your house and related to its interior. By adding an exterior deck to the side of an interior room, you extend that room's purpose to the garden. You make your house feel bigger, and you link inside to outside in a useful way.

The ideal deck looks best when it holds people above a nearby landscape that slopes down and away from it: open woodland that slopes to the edge of a stream or lake, bedrock at the shore of a lake or the coastline of an ocean, the edge of a hillside.

Having said that, most of us don't have property with such dramatic landscapes sloping away from our gardens, so we build decks that hold people three feet above flat lawn. Before going on to look at two alternatives of how you can make ordinary decks over ordinary lawn come to life, let's look at two decks that do hold people above dramatic landscapes so you can see really dramatic decks at work.

Out and Over the Pacific Ocean

The remarkable deck off a house in Carmel, California, that you see in figure 2.1 was surely inspired by the lines of the prow of a ship. The sweep of both deck and railing draws people to that spot and holds them there. And what holds them is the sight of an infinite and dramatic view from a little place. People like to see big views from little places. Just think for a moment about what you do when you go to the beach. One of the first things you do is make a little place for family and friends. You lay blankets or rugs down to claim a bit of the beach as your own, you set up chairs to furnish your little room, you push an umbrella post into the sand to give the room a little ceiling. You make a small place from which to see the big view. This deck does the same thing.

To see how any deck functions, compare the lawn below in figure 2.1 with the deck above to gain a better understanding of what roles a deck off your house might play. As you can see, the lawn is broad, open and flat. The deck—at least what we can see of it—is also flat, but it has that small prow and therein lies a world of difference. The prow encloses you, makes you feel safe. The lawn does not enclose, does not gather around you in the same way. You stand *within* the deck's prow held safely above all that natural wildness; you stand *on* the lawn at the edge of precipitous bedrock looking out over the wild sea. Stand on the deck and you have easy access to the comforts of the house. Stand on the lawn and you are downstairs and at a distance from the comforts of the house. Furthermore, because the lawn has to be mown and probably irrigated, any furniture placed on it will feel temporary; place furniture on the deck and it will feel permanent.

As you explore the contrasts between lawn and deck, look at their similarities too, because they hold important clues for you as you design your own deck as well as the edges of your own lawn:

- Both the deck and lawn are level, so they visually relate to one another.
- Similarly designed railing appears on both deck and the retaining wall surrounding the lawn; the railing, then, visually relates one to the other.
- The deck railing closest to the sea is free of potted plants so your attention remains on the drama of the sea; no gardens intrude between people and railing below so, again, the view of the ocean is the point.

The deck shows the drama of this site. Had the owners not built it but left the unpredictable and wild bedrock as the only surface on which to walk, people could not get near enough to the ocean to feel its drama. They would remain in the house, separate from nature, from the wild Pacific. This deck, then, is the bridge, the link between domestic and wild.

Figure 2.1: The best decks hold people above dramatic views. This deck directly off the living room of a house in Carmel, California, reaches out over the bedrock below to provide a dramatic experience. Spotlights illuminate the white foam on the sea at night.

By the McKenzie River

Decks can be connected to the house or be free-standing and at a distance from it. Roberta and Scott Bolling live on the McKenzie River near Eugene, Oregon. The Bollings are serious gardeners with an affinity for the natural world. Because they live within such a lovely garden that runs right up to the banks of a river, they want guests at their bed and breakfast, as well as members of their family, to appreciate both the tame and the wild, the garden and the river. They used a freestanding deck to act as a safe and attractive link between those two worlds (see figure 2.2). There are several principles inherent in this design that you might be able to put to work as you develop a deck at the edge of a stream, river or even woodland:

- By placing a woodland garden between boardwalk and lawn, the deck feels separate from the domesticated lawn. Sit on this deck and you feel you are in a place apart.
- That sense of the deck being a place apart is further supported by the fact that the boardwalk runs down a slope and then turns 90 degrees to the right for six feet or so. Had the boardwalk run straight from lawn to deck, you would not have felt separated from lawn and house.
- The right angle in the boardwalk is justified by the mature tree, thereby making the deck feel as though it has been there for a long time.

- The deck is cut out ever so slightly to make room for the trunk of the tree. That gentle accommodation for the tree relates deck to mature woodland.
- The two promontories on the two outer corners of the deck provide engaging places to stand alone and contemplate the running river.
- The flooring pattern of the decking boards adds another level of interest.
- By installing railing only on the river side, the view of the garden upslope from the deck remains open. This ensures a visual relationship between deck and garden.
- The railing is sturdy and inspires a feeling of safety, yet it is open enough to provide a view from chairs to water.

While both figures 2.1 and 2.2 show decks over water, you might have a much simpler slope through woodland, or a bit of bedrock that looks down onto a meadow. If there is even the slightest slope in your land with a view into even the shortest of distances, all the principles in these first two examples may well help you see how to develop a deck and gardens related to them.

Figure 2.2: This deck allows visitors to this B&B near Eugene, Oregon, to sit comfortably next to a garden and within just a few feet of the McKenzie River. Drama and comfort come together so naturally. Garden of Scott and Roberta Bolling.

Just Above Lawn

Most decks off American homes reach out eight to ten feet from the kitchen or sitting room door and are fourteen to eighteen feet wide. Railing runs around the perimeter, leaving one opening for three or four steps that lead down to lawn. Stand on 90 percent of American decks and you can see in three directions with nothing but the sky overhead. The result of all this openness is that people standing on such decks don't feel they're in a cozy place. It doesn't have to be this way.

As you see in figure 2.3, you can do several things to make your existing open deck inviting:

- Plant tall shrubs or small trees around its perimeter so as to increase the feeling of enclosure along the two sides of the deck and perhaps even along its outer edge.

- Install a bench as you see in figure 2.3 rather than railing so you use the perimeter of the deck in an inviting and useful way. Buy or make cushions for that bench; wood is hard. The fabric you choose for cushions adds color to your deck.

- Buy an umbrella such as the one you see here so that you can provide shade for those who prefer it over sun. An umbrella makes a deck feel much cozier as it creates a space of human scale under it.

- Plant hanging pots as well as large pots that can be set on the deck to provide color, fragrance and detail.

Above, figure 2.3: The Reisers, who live in Maryland, extended their house with a deck, separated the deck from the garden with tall shrubs and then furnished the deck to relate inside to outside. **Far right, figure 2.4:** Decks facing south or southwest become very hot on a late summer afternoon. By building an arbor over this deck, the space is made comfortable all the time. Crosspieces support lighting for nighttime use. *Design by Michael Bates, California.*

Arbors over Decks

As you saw in chapter 1, you can build an arbor that is directly attached to your house. Figure 2.4 shows how you can attach both an arbor and deck to your house. By combining these two built structures off a room at the side or back of your house, you create a cozy, enclosed space for entertaining that extends house into garden.

One of the key problems with decks is that too often the sky is its roof; the deck gets very hot and perhaps even useless in July and August. An arbor over a deck solves problems an open deck can't resolve:

- The arbor overhead, along with the railing around the edge of the deck, creates a feeling of enclosure and coziness.
- Arbors can support vines such as this fragrant climbing rose that throw cooling dappled shade onto the table and deck flooring.
- In supporting a flowering vine, an arbor enables you to surround your family and guests with flowers and foliage; they feel they are in a garden, not exposed on a deck.

Chapter 3

Freestanding Arbors

s discussed in chapter 1, an arbor is a garden structure that holds vines and leafy plants overhead. During the centuries, this single word has come to be applied to two types of structures that hold vines overhead: broad arbors perhaps eight feet wide and twelve or more feet long under which you sit, or narrower arbors under which you walk in gaps within a fence, hedge or shrub border. While the first acts as a destination, as a place to entertain, the second acts as a threshold under which you walk upon entering a small garden area or the beginning of a path. Because both have to do with drawing people to them, arbors, in both senses of the word, are important in helping you draw visitors to your garden along an intended itinerary.

Look at it this way: your garden should show visitors unfamiliar with it where to go. A well-conceived garden design has an articulate itinerary. It might start off the back terrace or deck of your house, lead to an arbor set among trees at the back of your garden, then lead from the arbor on a stone path through a bit of woodland, come out at a stone sitting area with a view back to your garden and then move through other paths to other destinations.

A good garden is held together by a clear itinerary, and rose-covered arbors that arch over gates, for example, act as thresholds, as important passageways along that itinerary. Arched arbors in fences act as magnets that draw visitors to them just as arbors that shelter a sitting area do. The former is a threshold for passing through; the latter is a stopping off point, a place to sit, rest and gather before moving along an itinerary.

There is one last point that is central to the successful placement of an arbor, whichever definition you use: arbors need jobs. Arbors hold plants back or above so you can pass through. If you place a narrow arbor or even an arbor for sitting in the middle of the lawn and plant a few impatiens around the base of the uprights, it won't ever look right. Arbors need to hold vines above or shrubs back so you can walk through or sit under them. Use an arbor in this way and it will feel right in its placement.

Arbors over Sitting Areas

AN ARBOR AS AN EXTENSION OF A DECK. In chapter 2, I explored the nature of a deck and how it extends house into garden. In figure 3.1 you can see how an arbor extends the role of a deck even further into the garden. Look closely at this photograph and you will see the progression Mary-Kate Mackey followed off the back of her house in Eugene, Oregon. (As you read what follows, think about your own deck or patio off the back of your own house.)

Once Mackey installed the deck you see in the photograph, she then built steps off that deck to lead into the garden. Next, she paved a broad stone landing at the base of those steps and then installed a grape arbor over that stonework, thereby turning a stone landing into a shaded sitting area. Deck provides sun; arbor provides shade.

In bringing her garden right up to the edge of the deck and both sides of the arbor, she can sit on the deck or under the arbor and feel that she is in a garden. Lawn sweeps up to the stone landing but does not leap over it and continue by the deck. The result is that this grape arbor remains in the garden.

Mackey also takes advantage of the fact that the vertical supports for the upper crosspieces of her arbor frame important views: the two uprights behind the teak bench to the right frame views from the dining table into the nearby garden; the pair of supports at the other end of the arbor frame a view of the hammock and the gardens beyond. From the lawn, the arbor and uprights frame a broad view of the deck and thereby act almost like a portal. Finally, when on the deck, one can look back to see the balance of Mackey's garden framed by the entire arbor.

Figure 3.1: If you have a deck, extending it further into your garden in the form of a grape arbor with stone paving under it will provide you with the shade and enclosure you need for an outdoor dining area. Plant on two sides of the arbor and the outside of the deck and you'll be surrounded by a garden. *Mary-Kate Mackey Garden, Eugene, Oregon.*

ARBOR AS DESTINATION. Whereas Mary-Kate Mackey's arbor acts as both destination and portal, this arbor in Roger Waynick's garden in Brentwood, Tennessee, acts solely as a destination (see figure 3.2). His arbor, set into a corner of a fenced garden area not far from a neighbor's house, is made private and secluded in a number of ways. The six-foot-high board fence, the material of which echoes the color of the wooden arbor, provides the first level of privacy. The horizontal arbor decking increases the sense of privacy by creating what all arbors create—a feeling of being within a space and under a roof, albeit an open one. Exterior beams for the upper crosspieces of the arbor support the weight of a number of potted ferns that further enclose the space and break up views of the neighbor's house.

The result of all these design elements, along with the arbor being surrounded by a garden, gives anyone having lunch under it the feeling of being in an oasis, a place apart. The fact that you have to take one step up onto the stone terrace under this arbor only serves to support the feeling of seclusion.

If you look ever so closely at the underside of the perimeter beam on the upper deck, you will see rows of glass globes strung together with wire. These are small lights that, when lit in the evening, will suffuse this arbor/dining area in a pool of light, further enhancing that feeling of being in a special place.

ARBORS ANCHOR TERRACES. Once you find just the right place for an arbor—whether it be in the back corner of your garden, under a group of trees, against an existing or new fence or group of shrubs, or even off the back wall of your house, as you saw in the example in chapter 1—you can use the stone or brick paved area under it as a shaded sitting area. Over time you can expand that same paving into an adjacent area.

Gay Barclay, the designer of this arbor and garden in figure 3.3, did just that, and for a very specific reason. She and her husband, Albert, lived for years atop a hill with grand views down to the Potomac River. When huge houses began to sprout in the fields between their hilltop home and the river, Gay started to move her entire garden down the hill to a place where she could control views. She used this arbor not only to help her create the core of an outdoor living room, but also to provide the room, one that got very hot in the summer sun, with cooling shade. Circumstances forced her to change her outward-looking garden inward, and the arbor was just the right structure to help her do that.

Figure 3.3 shows how to extend the paved sitting area directly under any arbor you might build in your garden out beyond its edges. While other photos in this chapter have shown you how to extend the paved area under the arbor into paths, this one shows you

Above, figure 3.2: Any corner of your property where a wall or fence creates a place for an arbor might be a good spot for an outdoor dining area, especially if some part of the arbor can be seen from the house so the structure draws people from house into garden. *Garden of Roger Waynick, Brentwood, Tennessee.* **Figure 3.3:** Dense shrubs planted behind arbors can screen views and turn a garden inward as neighbors' new homes get closer and closer. Colorful cushions, fragrant plants and the sound of bubbling water enliven the space around it. *Garden of Gay and Albert Barclay near Potomac, Maryland.*

how the paved area under the arbor can be enlarged to create a broad, expansive sitting area in sun.

That expanded sitting area can then segue into a path that leads through a garden or woodland and to your lawn. Where the path meets the broader paving—that is, where the two meet at a junction point—is a perfect place for a water feature like the one in figure 3.3. It could also be the perfect spot for an urn, a dramatically planted pot, a sculpture or whatever strikes your fancy.

A**RBORS FRAME VIEWS.** While the preceding image bespeaks enclosure and being within a hidden, woodsy garden, figure 3.4 shows how an arbor can draw people to open lawn to see a fine view. Every pair of uprights in any arbor, in concert with the horizontal pieces overhead and paving on the ground, provides a four-sided frame that captures and clarifies views into your garden or, in this case, into a nearby waterway. By siting your arbor skillfully to take advantage of the frames provided by it, you can create dramatic moments along your itinerary.

One other thing you might notice is the shrub planting to the left of this arbor. Those shrubs bring up an important point about open-sided arbors and wind movement. In old Italian gardens, designers placed the open back of an arbor so that the predominant wind passed straight through the arbor in such a way that the wind was at the backs of those sitting on chairs under the arbor. These designers then planted shrubs to the right and left of the arbor to concentrate and capture that breeze and force it through the open arbor, thereby increasing its velocity ever so slightly. In such a hot climate as that of Italy in the summer, you could sit in such an arbor and always enjoy a cooling breeze. It's a precedent you may want to build into your arbor if you live in an especially hot climate.

Arbors as Thresholds

ARBORS MARK ENTRANCES. Entrances are central to a successful garden design. *The* most important entrance in your garden is the one that your visitors and family walk through having parked their car and begun their walk into your garden and toward your front door. If you can see big areas of your garden from the front seat of your car as you drive into your garage or parking area, then you are giving up the opportunity to create that all-important threshold, that crucial moment when your guests leave the semipublic world of cars and driveways and walk through a garden entrance that unveils your garden to them.

The moment you plant trees, shrubs and perennials and/or a fence that separates garage and cars from garden, and then create a gap in those plantings for a section of fence and an arbor such as in figure 3.5, you have the opportunity to create a compelling entrance. When Derek Fell, a photographer, took this photograph, he was standing near a garage accessed directly off a street in Naples, Florida. The arbor you see is placed at the beginning of a path that connects the area at the front of the garage to the front door. Traffic was passing behind Derek Fell's back as he took this photograph, yet imagine that just on the other side of this arbor and vine is the calm and peace of an entry garden shaded by palm trees.

So how is an arbor such as this different from a gate? An arbor, unlike a gate, is able to hold the bougainvillea overhead; the feeling of walking *under* and *through* is heightened. Unlike a gate, an arbor, having a kind of roof, creates a space of human proportion overhead. A gate cannot offer that same experience because the sky is most often the roof over a gate.

To add a sense of welcome to this arbor, the designer followed tradition; he built a bench into both sides of its interior. The result is a feeling of warmth and welcome at this important threshold. That welcome extends to the lamppost and tiny white lights draped on the fence that provide safety and a lightness of spirit in the evening hours.

Left, figure 3.4: Arbors planted on only one side can screen an unsightly view in that direction yet frame handsome views in the other three directions.

Figure 3.5: Whether you live in Naples, Florida, or anywhere else in the country, an entry arbor set into a fence and festooned with a vine can help you separate the semipublic world of your driveway from the private walk to your front door.

ARBORS MARK TRANSITIONS. The arbor in figure 3.5 marks the most important entrance in this garden and so has a lot of visual and physical weight. It is painted white, the most insistent color in the garden. The shocking pink bougainvillea demands attention, especially as it contrasts so brilliantly with the white-painted fence and arbor. The depth of the arbor, the gate within it, the benches, the lamppost, the white fencing that provides context for the arbor itself—there is so much that draws your attention.

Not all entrances, not all transitions in your garden call for such a dramatic entry. Look at figure 3.6 and you'll see a much smaller arbor playing a very different role in this garden in Charleston, South Carolina. This is an arbor at a subordinate, not primary, entrance: the path leads from the front door and through the arbor to a path leading to the kitchen door. Even though the rose on this arbor throws a strong color, it can't hold a candle to bougainvillea. To further tone down the visual impact of this decidedly smaller arbor without a gate, the designer painted it black so it recedes from view. Every signal here is that this is a delicate subdued message of transition from one part of this garden into the next. It adds interest, a feeling of elegant entry. As such, it feels just right for its placement to the side of, not across, a major path.

Figure 3.6: Arbors along pathways define the act of leaving one space and entering another. Cover the arbor in this photograph with a piece of paper to see how much this simple arbor contributes to the experience of this garden in Charleston, South Carolina.

ARBORS REPEATED. In the hands of accomplished gardener Suzy Bales, free-standing arbors not only mark entrances but act as structural elements in her garden. You can use such arbors in the same way in your garden. Let's take a close look at what Suzy Bales did with arbors and fencing in this garden (figure 3.7).

First, notice that in the background there is a long, dark brown pergola running the full length of this garden that is covered with grape vines along its length. Bales used that long, straight line of the pergola to provide a logical placement for the white picket fence running parallel with it. She used the fence, in turn, to enclose a mixed garden of roses, annuals and vegetables.

To mark the entrance to this mixed garden, she placed white-painted arbors at the front and back entrances to send a signal from a distance that these two points are where you enter this garden. Had she not used the vertical arbors but relied only on gates within this long horizontal fence, visitors would not have so readily known where they were meant to enter her fenced garden.

By marking these entrances with vertical arbors, one of which supports a red rose, she is able to provide a repeated form in the landscape; foreground relates to background. These two vertical arbors work in concert with the white-painted fence to hold this garden within a simple, appropriate framework.

WHERE TO SITE A FREESTANDING ARBOR

- In the corner of existing fencing or stone walls
- In the corner or along a fence or wall in a vegetable, herb or cutting garden
- Along one side of a large perennial garden
- In line with but set well back from your back door
- At the end of a long, straight path
- In woodland, to act as a destination along a curving path
- At the edge of a swimming pool where its shade would be welcome
- At the top of a slope from which the views are particularly good
- Site a pair of them apart from one another so that they frame a view
- Where it will be seen from the important windows of the house

Figure 3.7: Suzy Bales, an editor for *Better Homes and Gardens* and a garden designer, used the same principle in her garden on Long Island, New York, that Andrew Pfeiffer used in a garden he designed in Australia (see figure 8.7): repeat the shape and color in two arbors across from one another in a garden and you'll create bookends for it.

Arbors
and Arches

Apply your artistic mind to the creation of unusual arbors and arches and there's no telling in what direction your imagination might lead you. Use these five images to stir your thinking about unusual uses for traditional structures.

Figure 3A: This arbor is a combination of sitting area and fencing at the edge of this complex shrub and perennial border. The gardeners at Wave Hill in Riverdale, just north of New York City, simply expanded the vocabulary of the fence to the left and right of this arbor to create a seat below and a rose-covered arbor above.

Figure 3B: Frank Cabot has been creating a remarkable garden called Stonecrop for years in Cold Spring, New York. This arbor surrounds a mature maple, but because it is above grade, air and water can still reach the maple's surface roots. The deck under this arbor provides an unusual vantage point from which to see nearby gardens while also providing a display surface for pots. Fencing and other decks lead from this central idea.

Figure 3D: Robert Dash's garden is in Sagaponack, Long Island, in New York. Being a painter as well as a gardener, Dash loves color. This striking yellow arch not only draws guests down this terra-cotta tile path but also strikes a strong yellow note in a green landscape.

Figure 3E: Susan Colman Braintree, in a flight of whimsy, used an antique apple-picking ladder to act as an arbor against which to train this shrub.

Figure 3C: This garden with its white-painted arch, which gives the illusion that there is another garden beyond, was designed by landscape architect Michael Van Valkenberg for a client in the Boston suburbs. The arch pops out against the dark green background of hemlocks and deciduous shrubs and provides a strong focal point. Put your finger over the arch and watch the garden lose its center. Here is an arch that leads your eye, not your feet.

Chapter 4

Gazeboes

An arbor under which one sits is integrated with the garden itself. Its open framework holds vines overhead that provide shade for people sitting on furniture under it. Chairs and tables beneath an arbor rest on stone or brick paving that often extends into nearby gardens in the form of paths or sunny sitting areas. An arbor's corner posts are set into the ground, thereby allowing vines to more readily grow up them; adjacent gardens often flow up two or three sides of an arbor. In many ways, you plant an arbor, literally and figuratively.

A gazebo is an arbor on its way to becoming a shed. A gazebo is more substantial and freestanding. Its roof is wooden, shingled and sheds rain. Corner posts that support the roof are tied into wooden beams and joists that support a wooden floor. You plant an arbor in the ground; you set a gazebo on the ground.

Because gazeboes are more substantial structures than arbors, they afford greater opportunity for decorative detailing: cupolas, complex rooflines, intricate floor designs below and rafter patterns overhead, lighting from within. Because the roof is weather tight, you

Above, figure 4.1: Gazeboes are for sitting under and looking out. By placing a gazebo at an important point in your garden, where views in one or more directions are really good, you draw people to that important place where they can appreciate those views. *Garden of Gordon and Mary Hayward, southern Vermont.* **Facing, figure 4.2:** Here, the uprights of a gazebo frame views to the west and northwest into the garden and beyond. We set two chairs and a bench on those view lines. *Garden of Gordon and Mary Hayward, Vermont.*

can set cushioned or finer furniture under that roof and feel assured that in everything but driven rain, your furniture will remain dry.

The key role for a gazebo is to provide a place from which to look into the garden. Whereas many arbors often face inward and provide a place to gather inside a garden, gazeboes by definition look outward. Place your gazebo where it will frame scenic views well beyond its edges—to a church steeple, a body of water, a mountain, cleared woodland or a meadow—and it will be properly sited. Or you can do as we have done in our garden in Vermont: place your gazebo so that when you sit in it, you look down a long, straight path into your garden.

Gazeboes Conclude Straight Paths

About ten years ago we hired our friend Roger Kahle to design and build a post-and-beam gazebo for us (figure 4.1). We wanted the width of the structure to approximate the width of the lawn path leading to it. We wanted it to have a gracious roofline that would be silhouetted against the sky to the south. We also wanted the gazebo to shelter a bench and two chairs so that at least four people could sit comfortably and look north, along the full length of the lawn path between two perennial borders.

In many ways this arbor acted as a bookend with our 150-year-old garden shed (figures 5.3 and 5.4) about 150 feet north of it to contain the garden. Whereas our garden shed acted as the anchor of our herb garden, the gazebo acted on many other levels:

- Its roof can be seen from many parts of our basically flat garden, so it acts as a destination for our itinerary.
- Its corner posts frame views in four directions: north into the garden, south to the meadow and hills in the distance, east to a meadow sitting area under three oaks and west (figure 4.2) through our woodland garden to a view of a distant pasture.
- It provides shelter from sun and rain; therefore, we can sit in the garden even when it's lightly raining.
- It is lit from within by a strip light running atop the central horizontal beam so the gazebo glows at night, drawing us into the garden after sunset.
- It anchors and is the concluding note of our perennial garden.

Gazeboes Anchor Woodland

In chapter 2, I introduced you to Scott and Roberta Bollings' deck by the McKenzie River near Eugene, Oregon (figure 2.2). Their gazebo (figure 4.3) is set into a woodland garden just a bit upstream from the deck and affords a lovely view back to their house (figure 4.4). These two built structures are far enough apart that you can't see one from the other, thereby preventing the feeling that the Bollings have overbuilt in their garden.

Unlike our gazebo at the end of a straight, formal lawn path, the Bollings set their gazebo at the end of a curving woodland path. As you can see from figure 4.4, this gazebo is in full view of many windows off the side and back of the house, so it acts as a destination for family as well as guests to their bed and breakfast business. Furthermore, it is the destination for the steps and path leading from the back deck to this woodsy garden.

Because this is a man-made structure in an Oregon woodland, it tames the woods, just as you would tame that little bit of woodland at the back of your garden. Part of that taming gathers around the pleasing contrast between the wild woodland in the background and the refined construction details in the building: the hexagonal layout of the footprint and flooring, the rafter patterns, the finial at the apex of

Above, figure 4.3: A gazebo set just into the edge of woodland civilizes those woods and establishes a relationship with the tended garden near the house and the wilder garden in the woodland. *Garden of Scott and Roberta Bolling at their B&B near Eugene, Oregon.* **Facing, figure 4.4:** The uprights from the Bollings' gazebo frame a view back to their house. No matter which of the four chairs you sit in, views into garden or woodland are also framed.

the roof, the dark green fascia board and step risers. These all combine to provide the natural woodland with a visual anchor.

This gazebo also provides the Bollings with a center around which to gather plants that will flourish in semi-shade: ferns, rhododendrons, azaleas, dogwoods and viburnums, among many others that contrast in a pleasing way with the woodland background. The path from lawn to gazebo acts as the spine of a garden and provides yet more places for low perennials along its sides as well as taller shrubs and small woodland trees set back from the path edge. In many ways, this gazebo co-opts the wild and the planted woodland into a direct relationship with the more formal perennial gardens near the house. This gazebo makes the woods part of the garden.

Obelisks
Focus
Attention

I f your gazebo looks directly into a richly planted garden of shrubs and perennials, your eye sometimes doesn't know where to land first. Obelisks focus attention. Being strong vertical accents in a complex perennial garden, they provide a center, and a place for your eye to begin to comprehend a gardener's intentions. Being such interesting shapes with such a deep history, they are also simply engaging structures to include in your garden.

Figure 4A: The wooden obelisks in this perennial border at Frank Cabot's garden, Stonecrop, just north of New York City, provide a repeated structural counterpoint to the many flowering perennials in this border while also providing support for climbing vines.

Figure 4B: This metal obelisk is a powerful garden ornament in this garden designed by owner Rachel Foster of Eugene, Oregon. In combination with the stone sphere on the other side of the bench, these two ornaments add stature and a sense of the deep past to this new garden.

Figure 4C: This wooden obelisk is a variation on the theme. By leaving a little opening on all four sides and then placing a quartz crystal inside, the designer added a level of mystery to this structure. The stone atop the structure only adds to the intriguing nature of this obelisk. *Formerly Kim Hawkes' Garden in North Carolina.*

But while the Bollings' gazebo is set within woodland at the end of a curving path and ours is at the end of a long, straight path between complex perennial borders, both frame handsome views back to the houses as well as into adjacent gardens and natural landscape.

Gazeboes Anchor Corners

If you have visited Colonial Williamsburg in Virginia, you will have seen how the colonists used gazeboes and other small buildings to anchor the corners of fenced garden areas. In many cases, these corner buildings were practical places for storing garden tools and the like. Designer Lynden Miller has taken a cue from this very old use of and placement for a gazebo in her garden in New York State. As you can see in figure 4.5, she sited her gazebo to anchor the corner of a fenced garden area. By siting the gazebo in this way, she sends a signal across a great deal of her garden that here is a destination, here is a place to visit as you walk through this garden. But unlike the two previous gazeboes I have shown you in this chapter, Miller added solid wood on three sides of this gazebo and then covered that wood on the outside with trelliswork. The result is that she can use the interior as both a toolshed and a place for a wicker chair with a cushion so she can sit in the gazebo and look out through its one open side to a garden enclosed by a fence. By painting not only the gazebo but also the fence white, she creates a feeling of coherence around the entire perimeter of this garden area, while also creating a striking white-on-white winter garden image, one that is in full view from many windows of the house.

Figure 4.5: Gazeboes, which anchor gardens in winter, can be infilled on three sides so the uprights frame only one concentrated view. *Garden of Lynden Miller, New York State.*

This approach to filling in one, two or even three sides of a gazebo might be of great use to you if you want a gazebo, yet you live in a densely populated neighborhood that lacks privacy. By setting a gazebo filled in with trelliswork on three sides at the back of your property (and with the fourth open side looking back toward your house), you create absolute privacy.

WHERE TO SITE A GAZEBO

- Where you have the best view from your garden into naturally beautiful landscape such as a meadow, view of the sea or mountains
- At the end of a long, straight garden path
- At a high point where you can look out over your garden, a fine view or along a stream
- At the end of a long, low, narrow garden
- At the point in your garden where the gazebo will frame views from all four of its open sides
- At the end of a curvy path in a woodsy garden
- At either end of a long stone wall so they act as bookends to a garden between them
- In the middle of one of four perimeter fences surrounding a square or rectangular fenced garden
- In line with your back door yet deep into your garden
- Where it will act as a focal point along an important view line (from the back patio or from an important window in the house)
- Where the garden visitor will come upon it by surprise deep in a densely planted area
- In the back corner of your garden, yet in sight from the back doors so it will draw guests into the garden
- Where, if planted properly, it will block an unsightly view

Gazeboes Anchor Decks

Sometimes you may want to enclose sides of a gazebo as Lynden Miller did, or you may want to extend the inside of the gazebo into the garden to open things beyond the edges of your gazebo. You've already seen in figure 3.3 how you can extend stone paving under an arbor into the garden; here is an example of how the flooring of a gazebo can expand into a broad deck.

In figure 4.6, you can see how the owners, Marty and Neil Kyde, who live in Bucks County, Pennsylvania, extended the wooden flooring of this handsome gazebo into a beautifully designed deck, one that is in full view from the house above. This deck over-looks a sloping woodland garden with a path that leads from the deck and down through that garden to a stream.

To increase the feeling of coherence between deck and gazebo, Marty Kyde repeated the hexagon and related elements of it in the deck flooring, railing, and the teak table and chairs. Wooden flooring, wooden gazebo, wooden railing, wooden furniture—it all feels so right at the woodland edge.

Figure 4.6: The floor of a gazebo can also extend well beyond its roofline to morph into a broad deck. The roofline of this gazebo as well as the other three in this chapter, rise from all sides of the gazebo to an apex. *Garden of Marty and Neil Kyde, Bucks County, Pennsylvania.*

Rooflines

The rooflines of gazeboes and other roofed structures are important design elements. Rooflines can be ascending and graceful or lumpen and squat. Too often rooflines in prefab garden structures for sale in garden centers are too squat, in part because delivery trucks onto which sheds or gazeboes are loaded for delivery have to fit within state and interstate highway guidelines regarding height restrictions.

Look back to chapter 3 and you'll see that the overhead crosspieces on arbors are placed horizontally. Look ahead to chapters 5 and 7 and you'll see roofs on sheds, pool houses, summerhouses, playhouses—even dog-houses are two sided and come to a peak; that is, they have a gable end and an eave side.

Gazeboes are different. Their rooflines most often take shape from the floor. Our gazebo (figures 4.1 and 4.2) has a rectangular floor and a four-sided rectangular roof. The Bollings' gazebo (figures 4.3 and 4.4) has an octagonal floor and octagonal roof while the Kyde's (figure 4.6) has a hexagonal floor and roof.

Now look back at the gazeboes in this chapter and you'll see that all but Lynden Miller's (figure 4.5) has quite a steep roof pitch. The gazebo, unlike many other roofed garden structures, gives you the opportunity to create some really interesting roof patterns and pitches as well.

Chapter 5

Sheds

A garden shed is a fully enclosed building with a door and windows. Unlike an arbor or a gazebo, both of which provide pleasant gathering places, a typical shed shelters tools and equipment. While most sheds are utilitarian, more and more artists and people who work at home are redesigning and retrofitting existing sheds or designing handsome new ones. Others are re-creating sheds for additional workspace, offices, studios, fitness rooms or a small overnight guest house. Whatever purpose your garden shed might serve, it can play a significant role in the development of your garden. Let's start by looking at two utilitarian sheds and how they relate to adjacent gardens.

Sheds At Corners of Fenced Gardens

Joe Eck and Wayne Winterrowd garden in southern Vermont; one of their passions is growing vegetables. The shed they built at one corner of their vegetable garden (figure 5.1) plays many of the same design roles it could play at one corner of your vegetable garden. The far end of their shed is a perfect place for a

compost bin as wide as the building itself. The other gabled end of the shed, and its two corners, provides two starting points for fencing while the sides of the shed generate the line the fencing follows, thereby enclosing the entire vegetable garden in a rectangle. Other interior fencing and simple supports for peas, raspberries and other plants run parallel with the exterior fence so all straight lines in this garden are parallel or perpendicular to one another. Old-fashioned coherence, practicality and efficient use of space are the results.

There are also a lot of lessons to be learned about the design of the shed itself:

- By putting transom windows along the top of the eave side of the building, and by placing the small window high on the gable end, Eck and Winterrowd provided good interior light yet retained a lot of useful interior wall space for hanging tools.
- The old-fashioned board-and-batten style of siding fits the utilitarian nature of the structure as well as its site in this woodland clearing.
- The rough wood feels right too.

- Placing the boards of the door on the diagonal adds an aesthetic note to the shed.
- The pitch of the roof is one to one; that is, the roof drops a foot for every foot of its length. Such a roof pitch makes the building feel light.
- They used the same boards for the siding as well as the compost bin off the far end of the shed so there is a visual unity.
- They used wooden shingles to roof an unpainted wooden building set in the woods.

To fully understand the power of this little building to anchor, center and give importance to this vegetable garden, place a piece of paper over the shed and see how this whole garden literally and figuratively goes flat. Without this traditionally designed shed at the corner of this hard-working vegetable garden, it would have felt lost in the wilderness. The shed tames those woods and looks after its garden. It is a dependency, a little building that echoes and is dependent on the main house.

SETBACK REGULATIONS

Call the zoning administrator at your town hall or local municipality regarding setback regulations—that is, how far your building must be from boundary lines—before getting too far into the construction or purchase of an outbuilding. Also check with the administrator about permit requirements.

Figure 5.1: A garden shed can be placed at the corner of a garden; fencing can come off two corners of the shed to enclose a rectangular garden. The practical role of this shed determines its practical, traditional design. *Garden of Joe Eck and Wayne Winterrowd, southern Vermont.*

Sheds, Fencing, Pergolas and Arbors Fit Together

Before you read this next analysis of garden and shed, go outside and take a look at any small building that might already exist somewhere on your property. Do you have an existing garage, a garden shed or perhaps even a small barn with lawn coming up to any of them? What Chrissie D'Esopo did with her shed/lawn (see figure 5.2) might provide many clues as to how you could develop a garden near any small building you have on your property.

Notice that she used two corners of her shed to generate the lines for fencing just as Eck and Winterrowd did. You can just make out the fencing running through the asparagus in the background and among the cleome in the foreground. But D'Esopo didn't stop there with built structures:

- In the lower right corner of the photo, notice a rustic cedar arbor marks entry into this garden of cutting flowers and vegetables. The spider web–like decoration on either side of the arbor celebrates this entry. Without the fence of the same cedar, this arbor would feel arbitrary.
- A rustic branch teepee, in line with the entry arbor, supports runner beans and marks the center of the garden.
- A rustic pergola draped with grapes off the far corner of the shed starts a view line that runs as a lawn path through the pergola, along the side of the shed and straight through their entire property on a north-south axis.

WHERE TO SITE A GARDEN SHED

- Near where the work related to the shed gets done
- At the corner of a fenced garden area
- In the middle of one side of a fenced garden area
- At the end of a straight path through the center of a vegetable garden
- Along the path between the garden proper and the compost/utility area
- To create a second shed to match an existing one and use those two to anchor either end of a fenced garden
- At the edge of a pond, stream or in association with a dock or bridge
- Against an existing fence or hedge where you can store tools needed in nearby gardens
- Across the driveway from a barn or other outbuilding to create a small courtyard between them
- At the edge of an existing small and practical garden; add a porch on which to set a chair or two
- In the right angle of existing fencing or stone walls
- Alongside a garage, barn or some other previously existing building

Figure 5.2: A side of a garden shed suggests lines for raised beds along it, lines that help determine other bed edges parallel or perpendicular to it. The shed helps with the design of straight-edged gardens near it. *Garden of John and Chrissie D'Esposo, Avon, Connecticut.*

Unusual
Treatments
of Sheds

Figure 5A: If the side of your shed lacks interest, place a framed mirror on the side of the shed and then install a window box under it. This flight of fancy always draws attention as visitors suddenly come upon themselves in what looked like a window.

Figure 5B: Here's a little rubbish hutch/toolshed that Robert Dash placed near the end of his driveway at his garden on Long Island, New York. He loves the particular yellow he used on the door of this hutch. He also used it on the arch that you saw in photo 3D. Don't be shy when it comes to painting color on built structures in your garden; Robert Dash sure isn't.

Figure 5C: I simply *had* to include this photograph in this chapter on sheds. If you live by a lake or stream, it's such an amusing, appealing idea to copy. This dinghy is in a garden on Stewart Island, New Zealand, where storms take a heavy toll on small boats. The owner found this dinghy on the shoreline after such a storm, patched it up and made an instant toolshed from it.

A Shed Surrounded by a Garden

When we moved to our house in 1983, the shed pictured in figures 5.3 and 5.4 was there. Farmers in the nearby Connecticut River Valley used this structure with its hinged vertical board siding to dry tobacco. We use it not only as a garden shed but also to anchor an herb garden to the east and a crab apple underplanted with hardy geraniums to the west. In many ways it acts as the impetus, the center, the core of an herb garden we have been developing over the years.

The sequence of design decisions we made and the mathematics we employed to support those decisions might well be a model for you if you choose to surround any small shed or outbuilding in your garden. These decisions can ripple out to help you design gardens at a distance from the shed.

- First, we decided that this small, rustic building should sit at the west end of a small traditional herb garden. That is, its materials, scale and practical purpose suggested a small, traditional, practical garden near it.
- Knowing we wanted to enclose the garden, we measured the height of the eight-foot-high walls on the eave side of the building and set two *Viburnum prunifolium* hedges eight feet off each end of the shed. They ran due east for thirty-two feet; that is, we quadrupled the eight-foot dimension. We left two openings in those hedges, as you can see in figure 5.4.

- We ran an arborvitae hedge between the east ends of the two viburnum hedges to enclose the herb garden.
- We built a grape arbor off the east side of the shed; it is as high and as long as that east eave wall: eight by fourteen feet.
- We linked the two openings in the viburnum hedge with a four-foot-wide peastone path that runs straight across the garden.
- We ran a second four-foot-wide peastone path due east from the center of the arbor to the center of the arborvitae hedge, thereby dividing the remaining space into a classic four-quadrant herb garden.
- Each of the four quadrants is approximately the size of the door you see on the north end of the shed pictured in figure 5.3.

Once you make logical decisions for garden design based on the actual dimensions of a shed, just as we did with our herb garden, those decisions have implications for the design of nearby gardens. For example, once we had accomplished all of the above, we saw that by running a hedge north from the viburnum hedge toward the corner of the barn that is just out of sight in figure 5.4, we were able to draw a visual, physical and logical relationship between herb garden, shed and barn.

Figure 5.3: A small shed or outbuilding can settle right into one end of a garden. We used our 100-year-old garden shed to develop a traditional New England four-quadrant herb garden and then surrounded it on three sides with tall hedges. *Garden of Gordon and Mary Hayward, Vermont.*
Figure 5.4 (inset): We brought yew hedges (as we have only a minimal deer problem) at a right angle to our *Viburnum prunifolium* hedges to visually relate barn to shed. *Garden of Gordon and Mary Hayward, Vermont.*

Two Sheds as Bookends

Artists Tommy Simpson and Missy Stevens have used their two diminutive sheds (figure 5.6)—the one on the left for sitting, the one on the right for tool storage—in a way that might inspire you to see the space between two small outbuildings in a new way. Being visual people, Simpson and Stevens see relationships and visual links across these two buildings that might stir your thinking.

- They stretched wires from the two corners of the sheds to support a green canvas awning that can be pulled back to allow sun to light up a dining table out of sight from the photographer. This awning can also be pulled into the position you see in the photo to provide shade. Of course, the awning also underpins the relationship between the two sheds.
- They used the back corners of the sheds to generate lines for fencing to enclose this little rectangular space and set it apart.
- They chose not to repeat the same kind of fencing around the perimeter of the garden in order to underpin the fun-loving nature of the space.
- Tommy designed the scarecrow just for the fun of it, and then they placed the cows and heart on the door of the shed in figure 5.5 to create even more visual pleasure.

- They paved the paths through this potager of vegetables, herbs, fruits, berries and flowers with brick to underpin the relationship between buildings and beds as well as to provide a surface on which to set a bench, table and chairs.

One detail after another is gathered in this lovely, unselfconscious, engaging garden, one that brings a smile to your face because it is so artfully designed in a space between two teeny rustic sheds.

Facing, figure 5.5: Doors of sheds are good places to attach ornaments, plaques or other decorations that suggest the spirit of the garden in which the shed is placed. The ends of sheds often provide a good place for stone or brick paving on which to set a bench and pots. *Garden of Tommy Simpson and Missy Stevens.*
Figure 5.6: A pair of small sheds on each side of a garden can frame a garden and provide supports for wires that suspend a canvas shade over a dining table in the midst of a fruit and vegetable garden. *Garden of Tommy Simpson and Missy Stevens.*

Chapter 6

Pergolas

s you design your garden, build in a wide variety of emotional and physical experiences so that people are engaged in a lot of different ways as they walk through your garden. Plants are certainly the central source of engagement and excitement, but structures play many roles in providing places for people to sit, gather and work from. These structures involve our imaginations in many ways.

Pergolas engage in ways that are different from all the structures I have looked at so far. Unlike arbors, decks and gazeboes that form sitting and gathering places, pergolas are made for walking. Pergolas are long, straight walkways made from several pairs of upright supports that are set vertically to hold crosspieces overhead that either are horizontal or arching. These deceptively simple structures provide many layers of experience.

Pergolas Support Vines and Frame Views

Bill Walker designed a pergola for clients in Junction City, Oregon (figure 6.1). By choosing straightforward dimensional lumber to create this unpainted pergola, Walker contained costs, reduced maintenance and did not draw attention to the pergola itself but to vines on it and gardens next to it. As with most pergolas, Walker used the crosspieces to support vines, in this case *Wisteria floribunda* 'Longissima alba', the flowers of which are best seen as they hang down from a support overhead. He also used the uprights to support other fragrant plants that do not climb in the same way as wisteria and need to be supported so their flowers can be appreciated at eye level: *Rosa* 'Graham Thomas' to the left, *Rosa* 'Collette' to the right.

While Walker left the central gravel walkway unplanted, he did design perennial and shrub gardens along both sides of the pergola so that when you walk through and under it, you are walking through a garden. (You'll see how this way of planting a pergola works even more clearly in figure 6.2.) While you can't see this feature of a pergola at work in figure 6.1, each pair of uprights, in concert with the crosspieces overhead and the ground below, provides a four-sided frame as you look to your right and left into adjacent gardens. The result of this frame is that you see garden images just as you see paintings: framed, defined, within a structure.

What you can see in this photo is how the end supports of all pergolas frame a view at the far ends of a pergola out into the garden. Walker took advantage of that fact and planted a tree in line with the center of the pergola to provide an interesting conclusion for the walk through this garden structure. He could also have placed a beautiful planted pot there, a bench or chair, or an urn with water bubbling out of it. There is no end to the ways Walker or you could take advantage of this and all the frames pergolas provide.

This framing provided by pergola uprights at their sides and ends is a very important element in a garden. When Mary and I were developing one area of our garden, we focused solely on plants organized around two brick paths crossing at right angles to form a four-part garden (see figure 6A). Plants and path didn't hold the design strongly enough. The day we put in the colonnade of black locust posts, we gave the weak garden a spine. And in setting pairs of uprights ten feet on center along all four paths, we framed and structured views between them. The garden came into focus instantly.

Figure 6.1: By leaving the uprights and crosspieces of a pergola unpainted, woody vines can climb and scramble as they will, and you won't have to periodically pull the vines off to paint it. *Garden of Bill Walker, Junction City, Oregon.*

Figure 6.2: This pergola is stained rather than painted a light gray. Stain requires much less maintenance than paint and so may be a wise choice for your pergola. *Longwood Gardens, Kennett Square, Pennsylvania.*

Pergolas Make You Feel Within a Space

Before reading on, walk around your garden and take stock of what is going on overhead and to each side of you. Take notice of what's vertical and what's horizontal. A well-designed garden offers a wide variety of experiences going on all around and above you; these experiences make you feel different emotions. Big open spaces, wherein the sky is the roof overhead, make you feel one way, whereas being under the branches of a tree makes you feel another way. Study your whole garden to see how often you feel enclosed overhead and how often you are exposed overhead.

Next, be aware of what is to your sides as you walk through your whole garden. How often do you walk into narrow spaces and how often are you in big, broad expanses of lawn? Do you provide enclosures such as arbors and gazeboes that offer both enclosure from above and to your sides, or is that experience rare in your garden?

Pergolas offer enclosure from both above and to the sides, and they do it in a way that need not be claustrophobic. Pergolas expand the emotional content of your garden. Look closely at figure 6.2 and you'll see that if you were to walk on the lawn to the left of this pergola, you would be in an area where the sky is the roof. You would feel out in the open. That's one feeling a garden can offer. Another feeling is just a few feet away under that pergola. There you feel yourself within a defined place. Notice from the shadow patterns on the gravel walkway that sun still shines under this pergola, but the experience of sun is totally different from that of being on the open lawn. Finally, notice that this pergola in the Longwood Gardens in Pennsylvania is more detailed than the one shown in figure 6.1. This pergola is painted; the ends of the crosspieces have been shaped following traditional patterns; crosspieces are more refined in their dimensions than the solid, reassuring uprights and overhead beams. This pergola, then, adds stature to this area while also connecting an orchard and a pool garden; the pergola in figure 6.1 is more familiar and basic, qualities the owners clearly appreciated.

SITE A PERGOLA ON FLAT GROUND

- Along an existing straight path
- Along two paths that meet at right angles
- In the space between a garage door and a kitchen door directly across from it
- Between the doors of any two buildings
- In the level lawn between two garden areas
- Down the path between two existing gardens
- Between the rows of trees that make up an allée
- Between two central lines of fruit trees in an orchard
- On the entrance path from a gate and running toward the house
- Down the center of an herb and/or vegetable garden, or around all four sides of one
- Running parallel with an existing tall fence or hedge
- From the house to the guest house
- To separate one garden area from another while allowing views into each
- From a patio to the entrance to an important garden entrance

Three Variations
On The Theme Of
A Pergola

Figure 6A: This shows a colonnade we installed in an area of our garden in southern Vermont. Made of hefty black locust posts buried three feet into the ground, this pergola without the top crosspieces, acts as a more open structure than the traditional pergola.

Pairs of posts frame views into adjacent and distant parts of the garden and support wisteria and honeysuckle vines. These black locust posts echo black locust trees growing naturally in the hedgerow just across the dirt road from our garden.

Figure 6B: This shows a metal arch/pergola in a tiny garden in Kansas City, Missouri, made to make the garden feel bigger than it really is. (The door framed by the far end of the arch suggests a garden beyond when, in fact, the door is fixed.) Arches made of this small diameter and lightweight pipe

are also visually light. They are far more transparent than wooden pergolas and so the beauty of the pergola itself is traded in for an inexpensive and easily installed alternative. A lightweight frame such as this can only support light plants, so runner beans, clematis and a self-supporting apple are all trained onto this frame. Kits for these arches are often available.

Figure 6C: Remove the crosspieces and the second row of uprights from a pergola and you have an arbor. Such an arbor can be placed virtually anywhere in the garden where a pergola might go. The only difference would be that you would walk past the arbor rather than under the pergola. An arbor such as this could run along the back of a perennial garden; around the perimeter of a four-quadrant garden; or enclose one, two or three sides of a sitting area.

One last point: if you look to the far left of both figures 6.1 and 6.2 you'll see how you can use pergola uprights to support trelliswork. Such trellis with vines attached further encloses the space at certain points along the length of a pergola.

Pergolas Provide Privacy

As our houses get larger and our building lots get smaller, the space between houses in suburban neighborhoods shrink. Privacy is at a premium. As you can see in figure 6.3, you can use the pergola, combined with fencing and trelliswork, to increase privacy both from the side as well as from above. There are several attributes that make this design by Patricia Larsen in the suburbs of Boston, Massachusetts, so successful:

- The lines of the pergola are refined and light. The scale of uprights is just a bit more substantial than that of crosspieces. The uprights feel solid and safe; the crosspieces are light, their ends delicately shaped to reflect the traditional nature of the house.
- The steps rise up this slope in accord with the change of elevation of the pergola; path and step design are in harmony with the pergola design.
- The fence at the back of the pergola also steps up in accord with the bluestone steps, thereby reinforcing coherence.
- The lower two-thirds of the fence is painted the same gray green color as the house; the white trim of the house is repeated in the white trim surround of the fence panels, thereby lightening the look.

- The trelliswork atop the solid fence further lightens the look of the fence, thereby preventing it from becoming too much of a solid, un-neighborly barrier.
- Larsen planted clematis at the base of several uprights so the vines could scramble over the crosspieces of the pergola to add one more level of privacy overhead.
- The use of gray green and white paint on the house generates the colors of the pergola, fence, trelliswork, bench and even the carved-granite foxes. Unity, coherence and calm result.
- Dark green boxwood hedges and lawn act as foils for white-flowering tulips; white-blooming *Fothergilla gardenii;* the white trunk of the birch tree; and the white in trellis, fence and bench.
- The panel of bluestone just across the path from the bench acts as an invitation to step off that path and out from under the pergola to walk across the open lawn to see the gardens. The carved-granite foxes support that invitation.
- The pergola is the structure that ties all these elements into an elegant whole by generating the lines of path, beds, bluestone panel—everything.
- Increased privacy is the result of all these details.

I want to remind you of one of the key points to keep in mind about built structures in the garden: they need jobs. They need a function, a real role to play in the life of the garden. If you install a garden structure for purely decorative reasons, it will never settle into the garden and feel inevitable. In figure 6.3 you see design and function hand in hand. You see a delicate pergola and associated materials and plants all in

Figure 6.3: Because white is the most insistent color in the garden, it demands attention and so is best used to show the lines of arbor and trellis when you want those lines to be apparent. Sending easily managed vines such as many clematis that are heavily pruned each spring along white-painted pergolas means you'll be able to remove them when it comes time to paint. *Garden of Patricia Larsen, Boston, Massachusetts.*

the service of making a walkway and pool area private. When good design meets serviceable purposes, everything feels just right. Give these structures real roles in your garden, give them honest jobs, and they'll look just right and fit in.

Rustic Pergolas Link Tame to Wild

The pergola shown in figure 6.4 and located in the Old Westbury Gardens on Long Island, New York, is meant to be rustic: black locust posts that still retain their bark support black locust crosspieces. While the tone of this garden area is made a bit more formal by a tightly laid brick path edge with lawn under the pergola, the rustic nature of this structure in combination with the woodsy feel of the azaleas and primulas holds the day.

If you installed a rustic pergola like this at your woodland edge, yet in view from your back patio or deck, you could use the pergola to draw guests from the back patio and along a path that leads under a pergola and into the woodland. The pergola, then, would act as a link between what might now be two separate worlds in your backyard: lawn and woodland. The pergola could, in turn, act as the spine for a garden planted on each side of it, as you see here.

Figure 6.4: This rustic black locust pergola runs through a woodsy garden of azaleas and primulas planted on each side of it. Because pergolas are meant for walking, planting each side of them means that people will walk *under* a pergola, between the uprights, *through* a garden. Every preposition provides a new experience in your garden. *Old Westbury Gardens, Long Island, New York.*

Chapter 7

Playhouses, Summerhouses, Pool Houses

S mall buildings help you design small gardens near them. As you saw in chapter 5, the lines, proportion and style of a small building such as a shed can generate a lot of garden design ideas. Even its door is a huge help; it shows you where the main path to the building should be placed. That path, in turn, breaks down your bigger design problem into two more manageable parts. It shows you where to put an entrance and fencing on each side of it. With path, entry and edges established by fencing, the remaining design problems for a garden in front of a small building are easy to resolve. To help you feel more confident, let's take a look at a few examples of gardens that designers and home gardeners have created across the country in relation to specific small buildings: children's playhouses, summerhouses and pool houses.

Playhouses

To build a playhouse and then to plant a garden in front of it is to start your child on a life-long road to gardening. In figure 7.1 you'll see Leann Olson, a gardener who lives in Coos Bay, Oregon, reading to her four-year-old grandson Benjamin. Leann built this playhouse so that it backs up to evergreen trees and thereby looks out into her garden. That is, the

building has a background, a place to snuggle up to. It's not out in a flat, open landscape, but in relation to mature trees. That takes care of the back.

The design for the front garden surely started with that brick path you see. It goes where it has to go: from Leann's house around a curve and into Benjamin's front door. Once Leann chose the position of the path and installed it, she then had two garden areas on each side of a path. She clearly knew how to proceed so that Benjamin would feel confident and comfortable in his garden.

They planted easily grown nasturtiums in the front garden, marigolds in the window box, a few foolproof shrubs here and there and, as you can see, they've got a wagon full of plants still to go.

The second floor, where there is a second room, is accessible from the interior and provides a vantage point for young Benjamin to look into his own garden as well as his grandmother's.

Figure 7.2 shows a very different approach to creating a play space. Designer Simon Fraser designed this children's play space for Jacquelline Clark, who lives in urban England. An existing brick wall establishes the back of the area as well as the two sides.

To separate the children's play area from the adjacent wooden deck where adults gather, Fraser designed a low retaining wall faced with wood. This step up retains topsoil for a soft and playable lawn. Fraser then designed an arbor overhead that supports a swing and gymnastic rings as well as a climbing structure set between two small boxy structures children can clamber in and out of. Narrow planting beds along three sides of the area provide places for children's gardens.

Above, figure 7.1: A garden at the front of a playhouse will put a child on the path to becoming a lifelong gardener. Memories of moments like this have the power to last a lifetime. *Garden of Leann Olson and grandson Benjamin, Coos Bay, Oregon.* **Right, figure 7.2:** Walls or fencing provide privacy and a background in an urban environment for a child's play space. The fence also provides a sense of well-being in that the child feels comfortable within his own place. *Design by Simon Fraser for Jacqueline Clark, Acton, England.*

Children
and
Gardening

The first thing you can do to involve your child in gardening is to choose a small limited area near a small building such as a child's playhouse. Develop a small garden area perhaps ten by ten feet. The south side of the building is best as it will be in full sun all day. As you see in figure 7.1, one approach to designing the beds is to run a path through the center of this space to break the larger area into two or more small areas.

The second thing you'll want to do is to prepare the soil. The key to success with any garden is the soil and how well it's prepared. And the key to your child's early experiences with gardening is success. Get the soil right and then create kid-size garden areas.

Raised beds are best. They are enclosed so your child can see the garden's limits. They're easily accessible from all four sides, and the soil preparation work is eased in so all you need to do is fill the raised beds with a superb soil/compost mix rather than have to deal with digging into and amending poor existing soil.

Once you have the bed layout designed, made and backfilled, the next step is to involve your child in the selection of seeds and plants. Rather than ask your child what vegetables and flowers she likes,

a question that might elicit hard-to-grow plants, do some homework ahead of time. Write a list of those plants that are easy to grow and have her choose plants from that list.

When our son Nate was a boy, we planted edible podded peas, carrots, cucumbers and zucchini squash. We planted runner beans on wooden teepees to form a little house for him. These vegetables can be harvested and eaten right in the garden, something that always appeals to children. We also planted fail-safe flowering annuals such as nasturtiums, marigolds and pansies straight out of six-packs from the garden center.

Raising plants from seeds is fine too, but be sure you choose types of plants that will grow readily from seed. Don't try sweet peas; they require knowledge. Do try edible podded peas, but get them started as soon as the soil is workable in early spring. Try beans and squashes. My point here is that if you launch into growing plants from seed, you and your child have to have the time, commitment and knowledge to pull it off.

If you find that your child is excited about gardening, explore the National Gardening Association Garden Shop Web site at garden.org on the Internet for good sources of properly designed and sturdy gardening tools for children. Provide your child with a hoe, rake, small spade, a trowel and gloves and she'll be all set.

What often happens with children, and with all of us, is that we are excited about gardening in the spring, interest begins to wane by late June and we've abandoned our efforts by late July when the weeds have taken over. Don't let that happen. Use mulches wisely to keep weeds under control. Mulches will also retain moisture in the soil so watering will be minimal.

Another way to keep up excitement in the garden is to keep it fun. Building simple, fun structures like the scarecrow you saw in figure 5.6 or the toolshed/dinghy in figure 5C will introduce playfulness to your child's garden.

Finally, when the zinnias are in bloom and the first small zucchinis are ripe and the cherry tomatoes you grew in big terra-cotta pots are ready, harvest them with your child. Bring them into the house and encourage her to make a bouquet for the dinner table and help cook the beans. Center the meal around the triumphs of your child's garden—one that should be totally organic—and you'll encourage her to become a gardener for life. Or, if your family can fit into her playhouse, maybe she'll invite you all over for dinner.

EASILY GROWN FLOWERS

alyssum	marigolds
sunflowers	impatiens
snapdragons	calendula
nasturtiums	cosmos
morning glories	zinnias

EASILY GROWN VEGETABLES AND FRUITS

beans	carrots
edible podded peas	cucumbers
lettuces	pumpkins
zucchini squash	strawberries

Figure 7.3: Trees such as these beeches that retain their shape after shearing can be used to create any number of living garden structures for children. *Bradenham Hall, Norfolk, England.* **Facing, figure 7.4:** You could surround a little summerhouse such as this with a fragrant garden. This structure is a playhouse for Carol Dickinson's grandchildren when they come to visit her in Rancho Santa Fe, California.

Fig 7.3 is also English. Mary and I visited Bradenham Hall in Norfolk many years ago and saw this playhouse for grandchildren made of beech saplings of both the green- and red-leaf varieties trained to a metal framework. The grandparents had laid out a table and chairs inside this living playhouse. Windows cut into the beechwood on the back and two sides allow light to get into this shady little retreat for children. Because beech is so readily trained, it is the perfect sapling to use if you want to create a beech house like this. The only thing to keep in mind is that you will have to shear it at least twice during the growing season. (I shear our beech tunnel twice and sometimes three times a year to keep its shape clear.) Being set into a woodsy clearing among 200-year-old oaks and beeches, the children can feel they are in a world of their own.

Summerhouses

These little structures are places for retreat during the clement months of the year. They sometimes have basic plumbing or wiring in them, but as more and more people work at home, many people are turning these small seasonal buildings into full-fledged workspaces with computers, sofas and chairs, the works.

Figure 7.4 is a summerhouse for Carol Dickinson's grandchildren in her garden in Rancho Santa Fe, California. Lavender blooms in the foreground while roses scramble over the roof, setting this sweet structure into the garden. I suspect Carol followed the same design process I would have followed:

- Given the symmetry of the building's structure, run a path straight to the front door.
- Enclose a small garden in front of this little house. Run white picket fencing from the two front corners out a ways and then have that fencing turn 90 degrees to run up the sides of the path.
- Pave a small area by the house with brick, and set a few chairs on the paving so children can sit in their front garden.
- Plant a garden of lavender and other fragrant plants for children to enjoy.
- Install white-painted trellis off each front corner of the house. The trelliswork will add detail to the house and will help show the rose where it is meant to go.

■ The paint on this children's summerhouse inspires other colors in the garden. The dark green paint used on the shutters of the house is repeated in the color of the chair. White windows, door, trim and window boxes suggest the color white for the fence as well as for white-flowering perennials. The gray paint on the walls of the house provides a rich background for the gray green leaves of lavender.

The role of paint colors in the summerhouse in figure 7.5 is very different from the role color plays in Carol Dickinson's garden. This brightly painted building and its colorful front garden are part of the larger Mullen Garden designed by Pamela and Paul Panum in Harrisburg, Oregon. Here, the designers used two colors of striking contrast to add a lot of zing. They then chose flowering perennials that would throw stronger color into this small, exuberant garden.

Yet the exuberance of this garden is all held in place by built structures. The fence is built parallel with the front of the summerhouse; the gate is positioned directly off the door of the house; the raised beds are gathered down the length of the path that runs straight to that same door. Everything fits: flamboyance contained. As you saw in the images from Robert Dash's garden (figures 3D and 5B), you can bring lasting color into your garden by using striking paint on built structures.

Figure 7.5: Small raised beds for flowers and vegetables can be aligned with any small structure in your garden to not only set the building into a garden but also to draw guests and family to it. *Designed by Pamela and Paul Panum for the Mullen family in Harrisburg, Oregon.*

Structures
with a Sense
of Humor

Playful yet useful structures
for birds, pets or people
can lighten the mood of a garden
and help introduce unexpected
color as well.

Figure 7A: This painted doghouse in the
Children's Garden at the Chicago Botanic Garden
has a green roof planted with portulaca and
sedums among other drought-tolerant plants.
Your dog deserves the best.

Figure 7B: This birdhouse in the suburbs of Baltimore, Maryland, is surely listed in the Relais et Chateaux brochure of fine summerhouses for birds.

Figure 7C: Scott Thurmon, who lives in Austin, Texas, installed this outdoor shower on a rooftop overhung by a large live oak. He gained privacy by growing *Mandevilla* 'Alice DuPont' on a wire fence as well as celosia and Hawaiian kalanchoe in pots.

The Outdoor Kitchen

One of the major trends in American gardening since the turn of the millennium is outdoor living and thus the outdoor kitchen. As I travel America lecturing, designing and researching for my books, I am seeing more and more outdoor kitchens. Some are set within summerhouses; others are within less formal structures such as you see in figure 7.6.

This outdoor kitchen, designed by Gay Barclay (her outdoor living room is in figure 3.3), is roofed with standing seam metal that is supported by rustic logs from which the bark has been peeled. The structure shelters a properly fitted kitchen replete with broad counters, refrigerator and stove. Setting it deep into her garden but right near her organic vegetable garden means that Gay, who is the one pouring lemonade, is able to prepare and enjoy a meal with her friends right in her garden.

Just as with her arbor, Gay extended the stone paving under the roof beyond its drip line to create a shallow, sunny terrace that steps down and turns into a path that leads into the garden. She then gathered planted pots around the base of the vertical supports while also using the corner post to support a vine. All these details fuse garden and kitchen into an unselfconscious easy whole.

Figure 7.6: Gay Barclay situated her outdoor kitchen adjacent to her vegetable and fruit garden. The two complement one another. *The Barclay Garden near Potomac, Maryland.*

The Pool House

The pool house is that place next to a swimming pool where people gather for a bit of shade, for a place to have a meal together or for a place to sit and watch children play in the pool. Given the purpose of a pool house is to provide shelter, shade, a private room in which to change and a place to perhaps even prepare a light meal, it is becoming a more and more complex space. If you look forward to chapter 11, you'll see the many uses of a pool house that the Granvilles and I put in their garden on the eastern shore of Maryland.

The pool house you see in figure 7.7 is headed back in a much simpler direction. This hammock house is somewhere between an arbor and trelliswork, somewhere between a pool house and a room for one. It is simply a place in which to lie in a hammock and be. It is also a frame through which to look at Litchfield Hills in northwestern Connecticut and valleys beyond as well as a sculpture, a piece of functional art.

Being pure white and made of such hefty wood, it stands out dramatically against nearby plants, against the turquoise pool, against the blue sky and the green hills and valleys beyond. You will better understand this structure if you turn ahead to figure 9.3, where you will see another view of this same property in Litchfield County, Connecticut. Hefty trellis-like forms are repeated here and there throughout this property to provide a kind of repeated form and leitmotif in the garden.

Figure 7.7: Pool houses don't need to be roofed and enclosed. This garden structure, based on the idea of a trellis, is an inviting place to lie on a hammock in utter peace. *Design for hammock house by Marty Wasserstein.*

Chapter 8

Fences
and Gates

s you have seen in many photos up to this point, fences work well with
other built structures in the garden. Thumb through this book and you'll
see a garden shed with rustic fencing that encloses a vegetable garden or
cutting garden and a children's summerhouse with a fence-enclosed front
fragrance garden. You'll see a gray fence with trelliswork affixed to it in a
delicate garden in New Canaan, Connecticut, and fence connected to each side of a
white-painted entry arbor in Florida. Look through the photos in this book to find all the different
fences in all those geographic areas of America. Fencing has one key role: to establish edges.

No matter how tall they are or how see-through they might be, no matter what material
they're made of, fences establish limits, and help separate one area from the next so each
has its own distinct purpose, mood and role in your overall garden.

Fences, in turn, support gates. Gates, structures we don't use all that often in American gardens,
are important built structures in the landscape because they mark important entry points.
When you walk through a gate set within a fence, you know you are leaving one area and

entering another. Gates clarify meaning. They also underpin all sorts of different moods; gates can introduce whimsy, follow tradition or be down right silly. But they always say, "Come this way."

Fences

GARDEN STYLE DICTATES FENCE STYLE. If you did go through this book, looking carefully at photos with fences in them, you would find fourteen different fencing styles illustrated up to this point in the book; there are ten more to come. Take a look at each fence and then at the gardens they enclose or the buildings to which they are attached. What you will see is coherence of style and mood; a unity between fence, garden and related buildings. Look back at figure 5.1, for example, to see a split rail fence enclosing a vegetable garden and running from the corner of a rustic garden shed; look at 5.6 and you'll see a playful fence coming off a whimsical pair of sheds; look at 6.3 and you'll see fence, trellis and pergola all working together with house and garden to create a private place in a densely populated suburban setting.

One of the most instructive places I have visited in my research as a garden designer is Colonial Williamsburg in Virginia. As you can see in figure 8.1, the style of traditional white picket fencing works with the white-painted outbuilding and well house and the white trim on both the brick building and main house (see chapter 11 for more on this house and garden). Colonial structures call for colonial fencing. Look ahead to figures 8.3 and you'll see modern steel cable fencing off a modern house in Washington State. Look to figure 8.4 and you'll see utilitarian wire fencing used to enclose a vegetable garden.

What you will also see in many of the photos of fences in this book is that they start at the corners of buildings both large and small. Fences start at the corners of summerhouses and main houses, arbors and decks, garages and sheds. In many ways fences are extensions of buildings. Fences take the spirit of a building's ability to enclose and protect and send out that reassuring spirit in a less concentrated way into the landscape.

FENCING DEFINES SPACES. Use fencing to define and enclose space and in doing so you draw clearer relationships between previously unrelated buildings. The fencing, in turn, helps you see how to develop gardens within the enclosed space or, at the very least, on each side of the fence.

Notice in figure 8.1 that the fence with gate in the foreground runs between the corners of a wooden shed and a brick outbuilding. By placing that fence between those buildings, the people at Colonial Williamsburg joined the two into a purposeful whole, something that you could do as well between one corner of your house and garage or between your garage and garden shed.

The far corners of both the brick and wooden buildings in this picture, in turn, give rise to more fencing to enclose this entire courtyard, one centered on the well house. The space between these closely knit

Figure 8.1: The gardens at Colonial Williamsburg in Virginia provide no end of ideas for how to join buildings to one another and to the main house with fencing to create garden areas within that fencing. While you may choose a material other than pickets, the principles behind where to place fences in relation to buildings is the same as those you see in Colonial Williamsburg.

Above, figure 8.2: Fencing based on trelliswork is useful in separating cars in the driveway from the back gardens. Make guests get out of their cars and walk through an arbor and gate before they can see your garden. *Garden of Gail Gee, Fulton, Maryland.* **Facing, figure 8.3:** Sleek metal supports and fine cable enable you to make safe, strong and see-through fencing near a modern house. *Becky and Bob Pohlad's garden designed by Steve Schramm and Jean Turner on San Juan Island, Washington State.*

buildings is defined. Rectangular boxwood hedges, running both parallel and perpendicular to those fences, confirm the shapes and proportions set up by buildings and fencing. The minute that you start to use fencing in this way to relate existing built structures in your garden, a whole new world of appropriate design ideas will begin to surface because built structures and the fences they suggest help you find the right places for plants.

F ENCES SEPARATE SPACES. For the past five years Gail Gee has been developing a garden in Maryland, one that I had a bit of a hand in designing. She has used fencing, which borders on trelliswork, to separate her driveway and the cars on it from her main garden. Figure 8.2 shows how she did it. What Gail is saying in putting up this fence is that when you drive up anyone's driveway, you still have on your public mind, the point of view you assume when you drive through traffic, stop lights and left and right turns. Gail wants her visitors to see her garden when they are out of their cars. Unlike most American gardeners, Gail wants people to walk through a gate and arbor before they can see her two-acre garden.

While this fence invites visitors in, when the gate is closed, it keeps deer out. Gail has installed utilitarian deer fencing around the perimeter of her garden and within evergreens and woodland on three sides of her garden. She then installed this far more elegant fence off the near and far corners of her house to join with the deer fence, thereby enabling her to protect her entire garden from deer.

F ENCES THAT NEARLY DISAPPEAR. The modern steel fence you see in figure 8.3 couldn't be more different from the two traditional styles I've just shown you. Here, a modern house on San Juan Island, Washington, drives the design for this sleek, modern steel fence. The rail atop the fence, the uprights that support that rail as well as the horizontal steel cables are all so thin that they disrupt the view as little as possible. Being so transparent, this fence allows for views through it and out to the view Becky and Bob Pohlad get from their house of Juan de Fuca Strait. Being sturdy, solid and firmly affixed to a stone wall, this fence provides safety for people standing near the garden and precipice behind it. Being steel gray, it visually fuses with the gray blue of the strait.

Above, figure 8.4: Wires stretched taut between cedar uprights act as supports for climbing roses and enable the Westmacotts in Stephens, Georgia, to enclose their vegetable garden with an attractive, semitransparent screen. **Facing, figure 8.5:** Espaliered pear trees following the traditional pattern of a Belgian fence separate two garden areas. This type of fence is perfect when you want to separate areas of a fruit and vegetable garden, in part because the fence produces pears. *Garden of Erica Shank, Amagansett, Long Island, New York.*

The fence in figure 8.4 is part of the Westmacotts' garden in Stephens, Georgia. It is virtually invisible. While you can certainly see the cedar frame of this arbor-like structure, the interior is comprised of inconspicuous wire suspended from post to post so as to support a climbing rose. This fence, then, is a combination of vine, wire and cedar posts all linked to the corner of a garage. This might be a model as you search for a way to keep deer out of your vegetable garden while at the same time taking advantage of a tall structure on which to display climbing roses or other vines.

ESPALIERS AS LIVING FENCES. As you saw in the preceding photograph, posts that support horizontal wires can act like fences to enclose or separate spaces. As you can see in figure 8.5, you could use that same idea of vertical posts supporting horizontal wires to grow espaliered apple, pear or peach trees in a fence-like way. Erica Shank planted five pear trees in her garden in Amagansett, New York, about eighteen inches apart in a line and then trained them to form what is known as a Belgian fence. As with any other fence, this line of trained trees separates two garden areas, defines the edges of both and could be combined with another set of five to create an entrance into a vegetable or soft-fruit garden.

You can purchase already-trained espaliered apple, pear or peach trees. While they require pruning every late winter, and often a summer pruning as well to keep their shape apparent, espaliered fruit trees offer an old-world way of enclosing or separating gardens that will also bear fruit for your kitchen.

Gates

Fences enclose; gates invite entry into those enclosures. Too often Americans don't use gates in their gardens; they feel more comfortable with an undifferentiated, open garden. That openness is not necessarily good design. The act of walking up to a gate in a fence, opening the gate, walking through and then turning to close it behind you underpins transition. These actions clarify the feelings of leaving one area and entering another and call up all those associations with thresholds, arrival and entry.

GATES IN FENCES. If you look back at figures 1.4, 3.5, 3.7, 8.1 and 8.2, you'll see that most gates are designed as an extension of the fence through which they pass; most gates look like and are built of the same materials as the fence. As you can see in figures 7.5 and 8.6, this need not always be the case. Here, a wooden gatepost supports a metal gate in a garden in Sharon, Connecticut. The design for the wooden gatepost echoes the wooden picket fencing in the background; the metal gate is a quiet departure from wood. White paint harmonizes the two materials.

If you look back through all the photographs in this book, you will see the color white on built structures time and again. White stands out against the red, blue, purple and yellow flowers in gardens, but it stands out especially against green foliage. White is a good color when you want to draw attention to the role that a fence, arbor, trellis, shed or any built structure plays in the garden. If you

Figure 8.6: If you want to send a signal to go a certain way in your garden, paint your gates and gate posts white so the entry can be seen from a distance. *Garden in Sharon, Connecticut.*

An Unexpected Fence and Gate

Figure 8A: Joan Kropf created this sitting area at a high vantage point in her garden in Eugene, Oregon. Steps that lead to this area morph into a low stone wall that acts as a bench. To provide a backrest as well as privacy, she installed a wooden fence. When guests are expected, she drapes a lovely quilt over the fence and lays out matching cushions, both of which, in concert with the vertical fence, say, "Come this way. The view is terrific."

Figure 8B: Marcia Donohue is a designer and artist living in Berkeley, California. She made these wonderful hand gates to welcome visitors to her garden. When you see these gates, you know you're going to have a wonderful visit.

want to clarify how a fence acts at the perimeter of a garden, paint it white. If you want to tone down its role, paint it dark green or let its cedar wood turn gray over time. As you see here in figure 8.6, if you want a gate and the entry it offers to show from a distance, paint it white.

GATES IN WALLS.

Walls differ from fences in their visual and physical weight. Whereas you can see through picket or trellis fences and espaliered or wire fences, you can't see through stone or stucco walls as you see here in Australia (figure 8.7). Walls are solid, formidable structures and so the design for gates leading through gaps in them has to be carefully considered.

When Andrew Pfeiffer designed this garden, he lightened the massive nature of this wall by painting it a bright yellow. He also broke the strong horizontal line of the wall's top by introducing the arch into the wall and then set a white gate in it. By answering the upward arch in the wall with the downward curve in the gate, he married the two materials while simultaneously forming a circular space that frames a view into the garden. By repeating the yellow wall at the back of the garden and infilling the arch with white-painted stucco, he was able to draw an appealing relationship between foreground and background.

He also took advantage of the fact that purple and yellow are complementary colors and planted long-blooming purple-flowering agapanthus on each side of the entry gate so they would show against the yellow wall. The gate and associated path ensure that visitors come to this important entry spot in the garden where they appreciate this vivid color contrast. Gates provide crucial entry points in our gardens, and they need to be planted accordingly.

FREESTANDING GATES.

As you can see in figure 8.8, gates don't always have to relate to fences. In this garden in Victoria, Australia, the designer has set a gate and its gateposts along a straight, narrow woodland path. To provide logic to its placement, however, she added a substantial boxwood shrub on each side of the gate to provide it with just enough of a reason to be there along the path. Without those two boxwoods, the gate's placement would have felt arbitrary.

Herein lies an important lesson regarding the appropriate placement of gates. As with all garden structures, they need a reason to be where they are. They need appropriate, unselfconscious roles. The job of this gate is to separate two areas of this one garden, to provide an incident, a passageway and threshold along a straight path. Had the designer painted this gate white, it would be too obvious; it would contrast too stridently with nearby plants. This gate quietly separates two areas of a peaceful woodland garden. By painting it brown, it recedes from view, it does not draw undue attention to itself and becomes a part of the gardens in which it is placed. Furthermore, the downward arc of the top crosspiece adds just that layer of softness and refinement to this gate; a horizontal crosspiece would have run the risk of being too severe.

Figure 8.7: Painting a stucco wall yellow and a gate white in the foreground and then repeating that same color combination in the background creates a simple unity in any garden. See Suzy Bales' garden in figure 3.7; she used this same principle. *Garden designed in Australia by Andrew Pfeiffer.* **Figure 8.8 (inset):** Setting gates at important junctures in your paths helps increase the feeling of leaving one area and entering another. Gates can gently or dramatically mark thresholds and transitions. This gate is in a garden in Victoria, Australia.

Chapter 9

Trellises

A trellis is a structure of light bars of wood or metal that cross to form open squares. That openwork, in turn, enables vines to curl around or hold onto the trellis as they climb. If you go back to chapters you've already read, you'll see examples of trelliswork used in a number of different ways:

- Figures 1.4 and 8.2 show a trellis set into frames so it acts like a fence.
- Figure 4.5 shows a trellis set into open sides of a gazebo to limit a visitor's sight lines.
- Figure 6.2 shows a trellis in a frame set between pergola uprights to separate one area of a garden from another.
- Figure 6.3 shows a trellis affixed to the top of an otherwise solid fence to provide it with a light and airy top.
- Figure 7.7 shows a three-dimensional trellis-like structure that we might call a hammock house.
- Figure 8.8 shows an open gate with trellis-like infill.

Figure 9.1: If thoughtfully designed, the very shapes made by trelliswork can contribute to the grace, stature and beauty of any garden. Here black-painted and handsomely designed trelliswork acts as a fence and backdrop for this elegant garden. *The Lindley Garden, Eugene, Oregon.*

Trellis as Separator

The Lindleys live in Eugene, Oregon, in a densely populated suburban area. As you can see in figure 9.1, their neighbor's house is only about ten feet from their common boundary line. In order to gain privacy for their entry garden, the Lindleys installed a fence along the boundary line, the attractive trelliswork of which looks beautiful from both sides.

Given that they wanted to be able to sit in this entry garden and under the branches of a very old evergreen magnolia, they raised the level of the fence so as to create a backdrop for an elegant Lutyens bench. The arch in the center of the main panel and the finely crafted bench in front of it, the finials atop the fence posts and the clean dramatic lines of this trellis add stature to this space, the core of which is that grand old tree.

Unlike virtually all trellises you have seen in this book, here the trellis is painted black so that its refined outline and delicate infill contrast with the white house in the background. Had they painted the fence white, there would have been nothing but visual confusion.

The elegant lines of trellis and bench are supported by those of the low linear boxwood hedges, the repetition of the three upright arborvitae off each end of the bench and the architectural use of cut stone to form a walkway from entry path to bench.

What alternatives did the Lindleys have when it came to establishing privacy between two closely abutting properties? That is, how does this refined use of trellis differ from other alternatives?

- They could have built a solid six-foot-high fence but it would have felt aggressive; it would have loomed over the neighbors' house and the walkway along its side.
- They could have built the trelliswork fence as shown and then added an arbor over the bench. One downside of this is that the attractive overarching branches of the aged magnolia would be much less apparent when sitting on the bench. Those same branches would make the role of an overhead structure redundant anyway.
- They could have planted a hedge of arborvitae along the entire property line. This too would have appeared un-neighborly and heavy, and the roots of a hedge might eventually break up the retaining wall holding up the levels of the Lindleys' garden.

The trelliswork fence was clearly the best choice in this situation. It offers grace, a sense of detail and formality, a place for a fine bench, and it acts as a backdrop for both neighbors' gardens.

Trelliswork for Enclosure

As you saw in figure 9.1, a trellis can mark boundaries. It can also form right angles to delicately enclose a space. Look carefully at figure 9.2 and you'll see a four-foot-high stone wall just behind the two chairs in this enclosed garden. Wanting to create a gently enclosed space, and wanting to tone down the tall stone wall so near to this small sitting area, the designer installed trelliswork running parallel with the stone wall. The trelliswork starts at ground level and rises to about two feet above the top of the wall. Being this high, it captures more privacy from the area at the back of the wall and provides support for climbing roses that clamber up the trelliswork to create even more privacy as well as fragrance. The top of the trelliswork arcs up and down to add a certain grace to the garden.

Trelliswork also creates an enclosed area at each end of this space. The designer placed panels at right angles to the stone wall to form arcing panels of trellis that support clematis and roses. Trelliswork is perfect for this space in that it encloses the area without blocking views of adjacent gardens.

TRELLISWORK LINKING TWO BUILDINGS. A trellis can be both as delicate as you saw in figure 9.2 or it can be bold and architectural as you see in figure 9.3. Architect Alfredo Devido used a big, bold white trellis in this Connecticut garden to pull two previously unrelated buildings into a sound relationship with one another while at the same time separating driveway and parking from garden. Too often we don't take advantage of the fact that fencing and, in this case, trelliswork, can stretch between the corners of two buildings in order to define the edges of and purpose for areas on each side of it. After all, the purpose of a parking area and a private garden are very different. But unlike the tighter trelliswork in Gail Gee's garden (figure 8.2) that visually separates driveway from garden, this trellis physically separates the two but at the same time provides many three-foot square windows that frame views into the garden.

In figure 9.3 a trellis runs parallel with the one wall of a garage and reaches out to establish a previously undefined relationship with the caretaker's house. At other places on this rural and expansive property, this same style of trellis in different dimensions connects several other buildings to form what feels like a little village. Devido also used a trellis to form the basis for the bold white hammock house in figure 7.7.

Facing, figure 9.2: Trelliswork can also be painted light green so that it quietly settles into the garden and provides just a touch of enclosure and intimacy. *The Diana Ross Garden.*

Above, figure 9.3: Bold trelliswork separates the parking area from the main garden and sets up a theme that repeats throughout the garden. See figure 7.7 for a trelliswork structure by the pool on this same property. *Garden in Litchfield County, Connecticut; architect, Alfredo Devido.*

Trellises Affixed to Walls

A trellis is the most two-dimensional of all built structures in the garden and so can be readily affixed to walls, where it can support annual as well as perennial and woody vines. As you can see in figure 9.4, designer Kathryn Barlow affixed this simple trellis to an old stucco wall onto which variegated-leaved euonymus was already climbing. By placing the trellis atop the euonymus and then training *Rosa* 'New Dawn' onto it, she created a sophisticated old-world look with four layers: rose, trellis, euonymus, stucco wall. The image works so well because whites and off-whites hold these four layers of meaning within a single theme. The trellis provides structure, the wall provides backdrop and the old door leads into the house. This is very successful design in part because it is so unselfconscious.

Arbors, Trellises and Lighting

Swimming pools are places where you can feel exposed, even if you don't have neighbors nearby. Swimming pools are places to relax, to lie in the sun, to cool off in the water. One problem with many pools, however, is that they are too exposed. Figure 9.5 shows how one family from the North Shore of Long Island, New York, increased privacy by designing a long, narrow raised bed that enabled them to separate themselves from the woodland and neighbors at the back. They extended the framework for those bed supports upward at both the front and back and in order to support an overhead arbor eight feet above the stone surround of the pool. If you look closely you'll see the black downlights affixed to the arbor just where uprights meet crosspieces.

To add that final layer of separation from the natural world behind, they installed trelliswork to the back upright posts. Over time, vines will climb both the uprights and the trellis to create a colorful and fragrant screen.

Facing, figure 9.4: Stucco walls, trellis, climbing euonymus and climbing roses all join together in a simple yet sophisticated way to
impart old-world charm to this entry to a home in suburban Connecticut. *Designer Kathryn Barlow for a garden in Litchfield County, Connecticut.*

Above, figure 9.5: Trelliswork encloses the area around a swimming pool for increased privacy. The trellis, in turn, supports vines to further increase
separation from nearby neighbors. *Garden on the North Shore of Long Island, New York.*

Figure 10.1: The bridge and dramatic plantings that define the movement of the wind draw people from the east deck of the house and across lawn and driveway to this pond on a hilltop property in southern Vermont. *Garden of Neil and Kathy Thompson, southern Vermont; designed by Gordon Hayward; bridge design and construction by Scott Henry.*

Chapter 10

Bridges

B ridges are irresistible. They enable you to walk over water, over low wet spots, boggy soil and other inhospitable places. They also help you draw relationships between garden areas off either end of your bridge. A bridge is a passageway, a threshold, a means of leaving one garden area and walking over a soggy or boggy place to enter a second. Without bridges, water and muddy areas are barriers. Bridges allow you to get near water and boggy areas, thereby adding yet another dimension to your garden. And because a bridge is often a beautiful spanning structure, it stands in pleasing contrast to some of the wilder areas of the garden. A beautifully constructed object lies in close proximity to the wild; one enhances the other in a way that is true for the bridge more than any other built structure in the garden.

A Bridge over a Pond
Neil and Kathy Thompson have a home in southern Vermont, one with remarkable views to the east, as you can see in figure 10.1. This pond, across the driveway from their house, was certainly nice to look at but only when we installed the garden did

the pond really become an interesting place to sit near or explore. Knowing Kathy would enjoy sitting in a garden by her pond, I designed sitting areas on both the east and west sides and linked them with a peastone path so she and guests could explore the entire perimeter of the pond and garden and then sit within the garden. But it was the bridge across the narrow part of this hourglass-shaped pond that really did the trick.

Unlike the peastone path that takes people *around* the pond, the wooden bridge is a path that takes people *over* it while at the same time linking the two sitting areas. Furthermore, the arch in this thirty-two-foot-long bridge as well as the criss-cross detailing under its railing can all be seen from the kitchen window and east deck of the house against the backdrop of water. The bridge, far more than paths obscured from distant views by plants, sends a clear message to come this way, to explore this pond, to appreciate the water, garden and views from this unusual vantage point from the center of a pond.

We chose not to paint this bridge but to construct it of cedar that, over time, has aged to a soft gray that echoes the color of the wooden deck off the east side of the house as well as the wooden siding on the house. Whenever building a bridge, or design-

ing any built structure in the garden for that matter, look to your house for inspiration regarding materials, colors, proportions and design details.

A Flat Bridge with No Railing

While all the other bridges in this section have handrails, the bridge in figure 10.2 does not. Given that this bridge is so short and spans a shallow pool, there is little need for the safety provided by handrails. The role of this bridge, then, is different from the others I have shown. Here is a bridge that is frankly a means of getting from point A to B. While it certainly holds people above water and thereby adds interest to the garden, the beauty of the construction and therefore its contrast to the wilder area of the garden is not the point here.

This simple bridge provides access from the house and lawn to the right and shed and pump house to the left. In providing that access, it pulls lawn, pond and gardens as well as buildings into a physical and visual relationship with each other and with the house. In doing so, it does not call attention to itself but lies unobtrusively in a richly planted garden.

This bridge, then, brings up an important point for you. How much attention do you want your bridge to draw to itself? The finer its detail, the more remarkable its design and span, the more atten-

Figure 10.2: This little bridge without handrail enables family and guests to get right in among the plants of this garden. This is a bridge that does not draw attention to itself but to the gar-

den through which it is located.
Figure 10.3 (inset): The large Magnolia grandiflora to the left of this photo provides a context for this bridge between tree and azalea garden. The color of the

bridge also sets off the pinks and whites of the Asian azaleas.
Callaway Gardens, Pine Mountain, Georgia.

tion it will gain. This little bridge is quite content to let the garden be the star attraction.

Bridging a Narrow Stream

When you see the bridge in figure 10.3 from a distance, you simply have to walk over it. Bridges *are* irresistible, and so become an important element of any garden's itinerary. This bridge over a stream at Callaway Gardens in Pine Mountain, Georgia, draws you not only to the grand *Magnolia grandiflora* to the left and close up to the Asian azaleas behind the bridge but also sends you into the woodland garden.

Look closely and you'll see that a boardwalk leads to this bridge. On the left, a gray boardwalk offers a safe, reliable surface on which to walk toward the bridge; on the right, you'll see that the deck of the bridge turns into a gradually sloping boardwalk that leads to more gardens. This relationship between bridge and boardwalk might be an interesting model for your garden.

A Painted Bridge

Here, on the other hand, is a bridge at Cedaridge Farm in Bucks County, Pennsylvania, that calls a bit more attention to itself, and rightfully so (figure 10.4). It's a beauty. Derek Fell, a nationally known garden photographer and designer of this, his own garden, told me "the red bridge is my design,

painted barn red to harmonize with the russet colors of autumn." I know he would agree that the color and simple, unselfconscious design of the bridge also harmonizes with the colors of the spring-blooming azaleas and the foliage of the cut-leaf maple. (Look back at figure 10.1 and you'll see how the colors of the bridge in the Thompsons' garden also harmonize with the russet colors of autumn in southern Vermont.)

Fell's beautiful, sturdy and slightly arching bridge leads across this narrow stream to a clear destination: a mown path and bench up the slope. As a garden designer, you need to keep destinations for your bridges in mind. If you place a finely made, beautifully painted bridge over a stream or wetland in your garden, it needs to lead to something commensurate with its design. That can be a beautiful garden such as you see here, with a bench in the distance, or it can be another built structure such as a gazebo, pergola or arbor well into the distance. That is, bridge leads to path, path leads to destination. *Design* a bridge in light of what it leads from, over and to.

Figure 10.4: Photographer Derek Fell designed this bridge for his own garden in Bucks County, Pennsylvania, to complement the colors of the garden in spring and fall.

A Finely Detailed Bridge

Place a bridge in light of those same factors, in part because as you step onto either end of a bridge, you look straight ahead to see where you will go next. Any bridge, especially if it has handrails, frames a view straight ahead from either end. Derek Fell placed the bench just up the hill from his bridge; I placed a sitting area just to the left as you walk over the Thompsons' bridge in figure 10.1.

In figure 10.5, Mary Anne and Dale Athanas designed their delicate white bridge over a seasonal stream in their garden in Guilford, Connecticut, and then placed a white urn directly in line with the bridge to create a relationship

between the two. Being white, both bridge and urn stand out against the greens of the surrounding garden and therefore show up from a distance. Unlike the unadorned bridges I've discussed so far in this chapter, here is a bridge with fine detail: white pineapple finials; finely turned balusters to support the architectural framework and handrail. Bridge becomes ornament.

Furthermore, this bridge gracefully introduces so many experiences, so many prepositions: you walk *between* the ends of the hedges, step *off* the lawn, *onto* the bridge, walk *over* the bridge and *between* the railing, and back *onto* lawn. And as you walk over this short bridge, your hand surely lands on the smooth pineapple finials. This passageway makes all the difference to this garden.

Bridge as Bench

Turn railing into bench—now there's an idea. If you have a place in your garden for a bridge, try this idea before installing hand railing. As you can see in figure 10.6, replacing railings with benches will only be appropriate if the water under the bridge is shallow or the area under the bridge is without danger and there are fine views from the bridge. If both are true in your garden, then turning railing into bench will double the bridge's usefulness.

Above, figure 10.5: The appeal of this bridge over a seasonal stream lies in its fine, restrained detail: the turned balusters, the frame around them, the pineapple finials, the unifying white color. *Garden of Mary Anne and Dale Athanas, Guilford, Connecticut.* **Right, figure 10.6:** Turning bridge railings into benches adds a new dimension to the experiences offered by a bridge. Those benches mean that a bridge is at once a stopping off point, a place to linger comfortably, as well as a means of getting across water. *Garden in Kent, Connecticut.*

Look back at the bridges in this chapter and you'll see that if you do want to stop on any of them to appreciate views into the garden, you'll have to remain standing. Here, however, you can either stand or sit. The benches on each side of this bridge add a whole new experience of walking onto a bridge.

There is another important point about this bridge, and that is its placement relative to the house and its windows. This bridge with its bulky dimensions and flat, broad benches is in full view from many windows of the house. The bridge acts as a signal to people in the house, or within the fenced garden next to the house, that they are welcome to come this way, to cross this bridge and to explore the gardens beyond. To support that idea, the shrubs on the house side of the bridge are purposely kept low so the bridge remains in full view from the house.

The fence near the house is painted white because the fence encloses a garden near the house with its white trim. The bridge is left unpainted because it is related, in the eyes of the designer, to the informality of the stream-side garden and the woodsy gardens beyond. Paint color or lack thereof sends articulate signals.

Bridge as Invitation

Because paths are necessarily horizontal and low to the ground, they often disappear from view. Visitors new to your garden may not know that you have made paths that invite them to explore until they come upon the beginning of a path.

A bridge is a path, one other element of the itinerary that draws people throughout your garden. Being a built structure that is horizontal and vertical as well as arching (figure 10.7), bridges can be seen by visitors from a distance. The result is that a bridge, unlike any other element of a path, can show visitors where they can go in your garden. The designers of this arching bridge send many clear signals with this simple structure:

- The fields and wetland across the bridge are accessible and worth walking to.
- This bridge is the way to get across the boggy area.
- The garden owners regard the meadow on the other side as part of their larger garden and the bridge is the link between the two.
- This constructed bridge centers your attention and introduces built order into the natural world.

Figure 10.7: A bridge can link wild to tame, wetland to the garden proper. A well-constructed bridge can make you feel that the wildness of the area through which the bridge passes is intentional.

Chapter 11

Putting It All Together

A Case Study of How Built
Structures Help Design a Garden

n bringing this book to a close, I want to look at one area of a
garden on the Eastern Shore of Maryland in which my client and
I used a variety of built structures to solve many practical design
problems. While your new or developing garden may not call for
all the structures or layout we used in this one garden area, the
role that a pergola, pool house, storage building, shed, fencing and even a bird
feeder played in developing this successful design may help you clarify your own
thinking about the role of built structures in your garden.

Susie Granville, her husband, Dick, and their children, all of whom are grown and
have moved away, live on the Eastern Shore of Maryland. Susie's mom, Timmy,
lives in her own house just a couple hundred yards west of the home Susie and
Dick finished building about five years ago. Just after construction began on their
home, the Granvilles asked me to help with the design of their gardens. As Susie
and I began to develop ideas, it became clear that the size, dimensions and proportion of her three-story house would have to be answered in the gardens by

small built structures we would place on this flat, featureless landscape. While the Granvilles have a lovely south-facing view across broad lawn and through a line of high pruned loblolly pines to the Tred Avon River and the town of Oxford in the distance, those pines and the house were the only vertical objects in an otherwise level landscape. Trees were clearly called for wherever possible. But it was also clear that a variety of small and functional structures would help us solve a number of practical problems off the west end of the house:

- Where would family park their cars?
- Given that Susie is an avid gardener, where would she store her garden tools and equipment?
- Where would she garden, particularly since her kitchen door is on the west end of the house and would therefore provide easy access into any vegetable or cutting gardens?
- Where could she have a bench where she could pot annuals?
- Where would the rubbish be stored for weekly pick up?
- When they install a swimming pool, where would the filtering and pool equipment go?
- Where would they store all the grandchildren's toys?
- How could we provide shade near the pool, especially given the very hot summer conditions in Maryland?
- Where might people gather for a meal or for drinks in a shady spot by the pool?
- How could the space around the pool be screened from view from the nearby driveway where family

and friends would park and where mail trucks would pull up to make their deliveries?

- How could the area be lit so it would be useful and safe in the evening?

The Design Process

The process that we followed to develop a design to answer all these questions and more is one I use all the time, and basically it's a process of going from the large to the small, the practical to the aesthetic. If the area I'm designing is near where people have to park, that's where I start. We also based our design thinking on the fact that the Granville's house is designed along traditional lines. Look back at figure 8.1 and you'll see one source of inspiration for the Granvilles' garden layout: the traditions of Colonial Williamsburg.

Here is the sequence we followed to develop a design:

- We sketched in a tool shed (figure 11.1) at the end of that bluestone path. The stone path visually and physically linked the big house to the little building.
- We knew that family would park near the kitchen door off the northwest corner of the house. We designed parking for four cars and placed a three-foot-wide bluestone path that family would pull up to along the front of that parking area. Family could then get out of their cars, walk a few steps forward and turn left to walk toward steps up to the kitchen door (figure 11.2).

Figure 11.1: The path from the kitchen door leads straight to the brick potting shed, a small building that anchors the far corner of the four-quadrant garden we designed with the brick building in mind (see figure 11.4 for the layout of this entire garden). **Figure 11.2 (inset):** Good garden design starts with paths leading from important doors of the house. Here the kitchen door and the steps down from it showed us where to run a path perpendicular with the landing at the bottom of these steps.

area off the east end of the pool. But how far south should the twenty- by forty-foot pool go? We would have to wait to get the answer to that question.

- We went back to the first bluestone path between kitchen door and garden shed. We decided to make a four-quadrant flower garden that would be just as wide as the west end of the house, so we placed a fence about four feet in from the first bluestone path and running parallel with it and placed a gate in the middle of that fence. That gate would be the starting point for a path that would run straight through the flower garden to a second gate set into fence on the south side of the garden.

- We then located the middle point of the west side of the house, which turned out to be right in the middle of a window over the kitchen sink and situated a second gate that gave rise to a path running east-west. The west end of the fence would show us where to situate the fourth gate (figure 11.4).

- A fourth gate became the starting point for a mown path from the main house and garden to Timmie's house in the west meadow.

- The point where these two paths crossed in the center of the four-quadrant flower garden helped us locate just the right place for a fine bird feeder, a built structure that would mark the center of the garden and center the view from the kitchen window (figure 11.2 again).

- We knew that a path would be necessary to bring people who just parked their cars from where the bluestone path met the steps up to the kitchen door. That path would best run parallel with the west end of the house yet be about ten feet from it to give us room for shrubs and fencing that would screen the air-conditioning units along the west wall (figure 11.3).

- We also knew the swimming pool would go somewhere off the southwest corner of the house, so we saw this second path, also of bluestone, as a way to bring visitors and family from the parking area to the swimming pool.

- We expanded the far south end of that second path west so that it turned into a broad sitting

Above, figure 11.3: This bluestone path runs between the west end of the Granvilles' house and the east fence. The role of the path is to draw guests toward the shelter of the pergola and the swimming pool.
Right, figure 11.4: The view from an upstairs bedroom shows the structure of this garden. Two small buildings, one wooden, the other brick, anchor the two corners of this four-part garden. Balance, not symmetry, holds the parts in a harmonious relationship with one another.

- We then returned to the problem of where the swimming pool would go on a line running north-south. We knew we wanted a garden on both sides of each of the fences surrounding the four-part garden, and we also knew we wanted a pergola or some structure to provide shade on the west side of the pool.

- We decided to leave six feet of garden space between the south fence and a broad area of bluestone on which guests could gather (figure 11.5). We then decided that Susie would need about twenty feet of bluestone for family and guests and that dimension gave us the placement for the pool—that is, twenty-six feet south of the south-most fence.

- We then used the west end of the bluestone to help us locate a small pool house where the pool equipment would be housed and insulated from the rest of the area that would be used for storing children's things and towels.

- The centrally placed east door of the pool house, in turn, gave us the destination and alignment for a pergola that would run east-west and parallel with the length of pool and garden fencing (figure 11.5).

The Design of the Pergola

For all of these design decisions to feel right, especially as they relate to built structures, they had to play more than an aesthetic role. They had to perform, to fulfill real purposes in the life of family and friends. To help you better understand how we thought about each of the structures in general, let's take a close look at one of them—the pergola—to see how it functions in the life of the Granville family.

- **Privacy:** The problem was that guest parking was roughly forty feet to the north of the pergola and the pool only ten feet to its south. By placing a garden surrounded by thirty-six-inch-high picket fence between pergola and parking area, its crab apples, roses and tall perennials would help separate the semipublic parking/driveway from the private area by the swimming pool. The pergola, being eight feet tall and festooned with roses, would complete the job of providing privacy (figure 11.5 again).

- **Access:** We wanted to show guests the way to the sitting areas and pool house at the end of the pergola. By placing the pergola in line with the pair of doors leading into the pool house, guests knew just where to go.

- **Shade:** Once the roses grow up and fill in more of the gaps between the pergola's crosspieces, guests who appreciate shade will have a place to gather near the pool. This shady area under the pergola will provide Susie with a place to set up a table and chairs so she can have meals outdoors.

- **Places to Sit:** People are different; some like it hot, some like it cool. The pergola divided the space between garden fence and pool into two areas, one for sun lovers, one for shade lovers.

- **Lighting:** The pergola crosspieces provide places from which to hang lighting. Susie chose black canister-like lights with many little holes in them. This way light is suffused by fixtures that throw a uniform dappled light onto the whole area in the evening.

Figure 11.5: Materials in a garden can underpin unity. Bluestone paths and white-painted wood knit all the parts together. Flowering plants provide detail, vitality, fragrance and pleasing contrast.

Above, figure 11.6: The summerhouse in the Granvilles' garden acts as a destination for the pergola; the nearby fence follows the same line as that of the pergola. All lines of built structures in this garden feel inevitable. **Facing, figure 11.7:** The vertical columns of the pergola frame views to the river or to the four-quadrant garden while echoing the straight vertical trunks of the loblolly pines. The horizontal crosspieces echo the long, low lines of the fence; the bluestone paths; the pool and its coping; and the water on the river.

The pergola also provided a number of *aesthetic contributions* to our design:

- The design of this traditional, elegant pergola with its fine detailing and white color has sufficient stature to stand up to that of the house, which echoes the detail and white color on the house.
- The view west down the length of the pergola showed us where to locate the pool house (see figure 11.6).

- If you stand with your back to the pool house doors and look east, you see that the pergola frames a view of a large bluestone terrace off the south side of the house; two major sitting areas in this garden are visually related.
- Just to the left of the view framed by the pergola, you see the bottom steps that lead to another kitchen door. We marked that line with bluestone stepping-stones set in lawn.

- That path helped us find a place for the grill just to the left along the path and hidden within shrubs and a yew hedge. The space is on the path between the indoor kitchen and outdoor dining area.
- We set two benches under the pergola for those people who just want to pull back a bit from all the activity by the pool. Pergola uprights frame views of the Tred Avon River (see figure 11.7) and the village of Oxford across the river.
- People like to see big views from little places. The pergola, under which people walk and sit, provides that comforting little place from which to enjoy the view. No other structure in this garden provides such a place of intimacy.

With the pergola acting as the lynchpin for this whole design, sitting there between garden and swimming pool, we settled fence, bird feeder and outbuildings into places that were right for them. These other built structures play many roles, both practical and aesthetic:

- The fence, the outer corners of which related to the garden shed and pool house (see figure 11.8), establish logical edges to the four-quadrant flower garden.
- The fence wraps its arms around the garden and makes a cozy inner space in an otherwise open, flat property.

- The fence acts as backdrop for gardens on each side of it.
- The gates set into the fence generate a cross axis that showed Susie where to place the bird feeder.
- The gates also showed us where to put paths so guests could walk through the garden to the pool and where Susie could make a path so her mother could walk through the meadow and through the fenced garden and up steps into the kitchen.
- The pool house, garden shed and storage building, all traditionally designed of materials that echoed those of the house, extended the architecture of the big house into the landscape in smaller, more approachable ways that help settle the house into rather than on the landscape.

These garden structures, along with all explored in this book, provide that necessary contrast, anchoring and centering that a garden, otherwise comprised of plants, needs. These buildings provide a backdrop for plants. They provide structure, line and framework for gardens full of plants and offer a pleasing contrast between architecture and landscape, between the geometry of structures and the natural forms of plants. The result is a balance between the yin and the yang, the natural and the built.

Figure 11.8: The color white, in both built structures and plants, draws this garden into a quiet harmony. Traditional design drove aesthetic decisions.

Appendix

Fence
Designs

hen deciding on the design for any built structure in your garden,
keep the local and historical precedents for such structures in
mind. By acknowledging these historic patterns in fences, small
buildings and gates, you'll underpin the sense of place in which
your garden exists.

For example, if you plan to construct a fence anywhere in your garden, you have
an opportunity to make the upright pickets (fence pales) reflect those historic
precedents. Following are seventy-two drawings by Peter Joel Harrison of historic
fence pale patterns he has discovered in specific American towns and villages.
Over the last thirty years he has been travelling across the country recording historic built garden structures: gazeboes and trellises, brick pavement styles and
fence walls, garden houses, well houses, privies and more. See page 151 for
more information on Harrison's remarkable work.

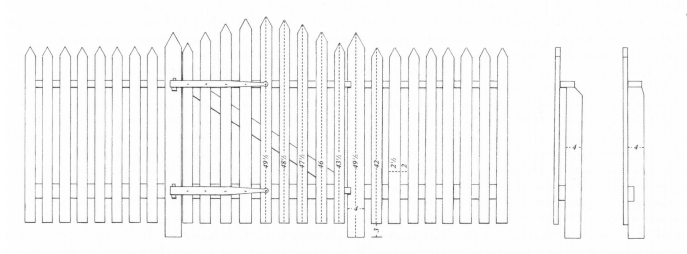

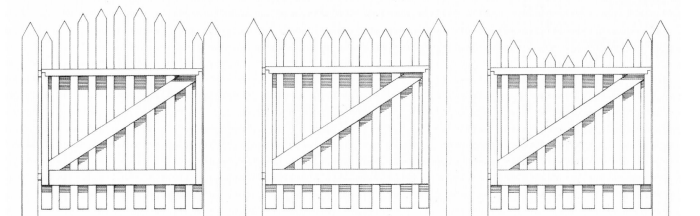

Colonial Williamsburg
Williamsburg, VA

Colonial Williamsburg
Williamsburg, VA

Old Salem
Winston-Salem, NC

Old Salem
Winston-Salem, NC

Smithfield Plantation
Blacksburg, VA

Zoar Village,
Zoar, OH

Sturbridge Village
Sturbridge, MA

Adam Thoroughgood House
Virginia Beach, VA

Colonial Williamsburg
Williamsburg, VA

Colonial Williamsburg
Williamsburg, VA

Old Salem
Winston-Salem, NC

Conent House
Falmouth, MA

Stratford Hall
Stratford, VA

Lloyd House
Alexandria, VA

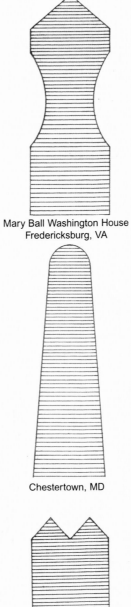

Mary Ball Washington House
Fredericksburg, VA

Mary Ball Washington House
Fredericksburg, VA

Cupola House
Edenton, NC

Newport, RI

Chestertown, MD

Cape May, NJ

Shaker Village
Canterbury, NH

Arch Hall
Alexandria, VA

Colonial Williamsburg
Williamsburg, VA

Mount Vernon
Mount Vernon, VA

Fredericksburg, VA

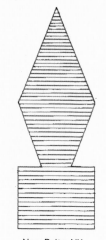

New Paltz, NY

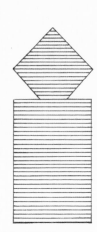

Colonial Williamsburg
Williamsburg, VA

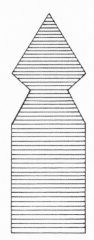

Palmer-Marsh House
Bath, NC

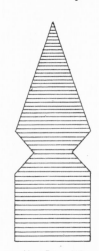

New Bern, NC

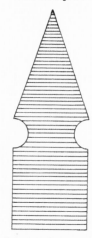

Frederick, VA

Colonial Williamsburg
Williamsburg, VA

Hill Hold
Montgomery, NY

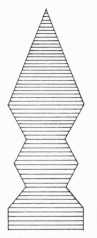

Mount Vernon,
Mount Vernon, VA

Mount Vernon,
Mount Vernon, VA

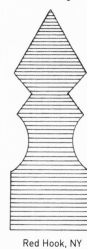

Red Hook, NY

Chatham, MA

Pennsbury Manor
Tullytown, PA

Grumblethorpe
Philadelphia, PA

Manomet, MA

Stawbery Banke
Portsmouth, NH

St. Michaels, MD

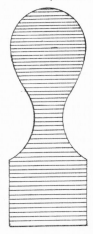

Westville
Lumpkin, GA

New Hope, PA

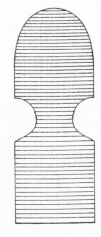

Shaker Town
Pleasant Hill, KY

Smyrna, DE

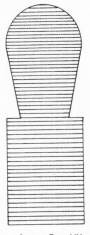

Oyster Bay, NY

Manteo, NC

Germantown, PA

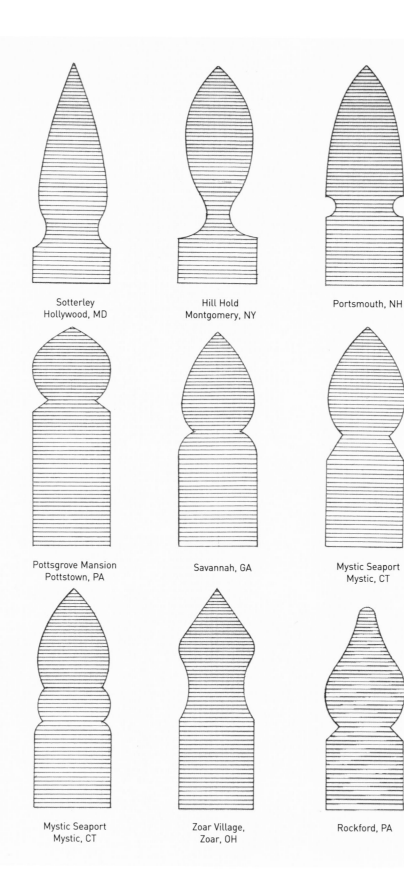

Sotterley
Hollywood, MD

Hill Hold
Montgomery, NY

Portsmouth, NH

Mystic Seaport
Mystic, CT

Pottsgrove Mansion
Pottstown, PA

Savannah, GA

Mystic Seaport
Mystic, CT

Trinity Church
Scotland Neck, NC

Mystic Seaport
Mystic, CT

Zoar Village,
Zoar, OH

Rockford, PA

Colonial Williamsburg
Williamsburg, VA

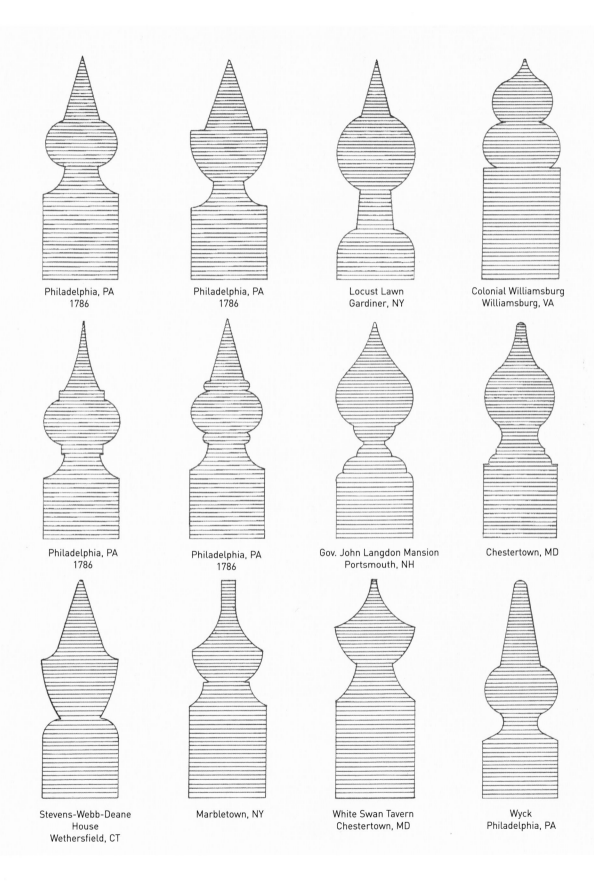

Philadelphia, PA
1786

Philadelphia, PA
1786

Locust Lawn
Gardiner, NY

Colonial Williamsburg
Williamsburg, VA

Philadelphia, PA
1786

Philadelphia, PA
1786

Gov. John Langdon Mansion
Portsmouth, NH

Chestertown, MD

Stevens-Webb-Deane
House
Wethersfield, CT

Marbletown, NY

White Swan Tavern
Chestertown, MD

Wyck
Philadelphia, PA

Bibliography

Atkinson, Scott, and Philip Edinger, eds. *Trellises and Arbors.* Menlo Park, CA: Sunset Books, 1999.

Beneke, Jeff. *The Sunset Complete Deck Book.* Menlo Park, CA: Sunset Books, 2002.

Better Homes and Gardens. *Trellises, Arbors and Pergolas: Ideas and Plans for Garden Structures.* New York: Better Homes and Gardens, 2004.

Brawley Hill, May. *Furnishing the Old-Fashioned Garden: Three Centuries of American Summerhouses, Dovecotes, Pergolas, Privies, Fences & Birdhouses.* New York: Harry N. Abrams Publishing, 1998.

Cory, Steve, et al. *Decks: Plan, Design, Build.* Upper Saddle River, New Jersey: Creative Homeowner, 2005.

Ditchfield, Robert. *Arches and Pergolas: Letts Guides to Garden Design.* Oxford: Canopy Books, 1993.

Edwards, Paul. *Pergolas, Arbours and Arches: Their History and How to Make Them.* London: Barn Elms Publishing, 2002.

Gertley, Jan. *Classic Garden Structures: 18 Elegant Projects to Enhance Your Garden.* Newtown, CT: Taunton Press, 1998.

Guinness, Bunny. *Creating a Family Garden: Magical Outdoor Spaces for All Ages.* New York: Abbeville Press, 1996.

Keen, Mary. *Decorate Your Garden.* London: Conrad Octopus, 1993.

Mulfinger, Dale, and Susan E. Davis. *The Cabin.* Newtown, CT: Taunton Press, 2003.

O'Sullivan, Penelope. *For Your Garden: Garden Sheds and Potting Areas.* New York: Friedman/Fairfax Publishing, 1999.

Smith, Linda Joan. *Garden Structures.* New York: Workman Publishing, 2000.

Stiles, David and Jeanie. *Cabins: A Guide to Building Your Own Nature Retreat.* New York: Firefly Books, 2001.

Stillman, Julie, and Jane Gitlin. *Deck and Patio Idea Book.* Newtown, CT: Taunton Press, 2003.

Taylor, Julie D. *Outdoor Rooms: Designs for Porches, Terraces, Decks, Gazebos.* Gloucester, MA: Rockport Publishers, 2001.

Truini, Joseph. *Building a Shed.* Newtown, CT: Taunton Press, 2003.

White, Lee Anne. *Pool Idea Book.* Newtown, CT: Taunton Press, 2006.

Resources

GARDENSHEDS

GARDENSHEDS.COM
717-397-5430
Nellie Ahl lives in Lancaster, Pennsylvania, and has a business called Gardensheds. She and her crew of six Amish craftsmen construct beautifully designed and sturdily built garden sheds Nellie has designed. She offers pool houses, playhouses, studios, small greenhouses and many other garden buildings. Because they make each building to order, they can custom design to your specific requirements. Upon completing a building, Nellie sees to its delivery to customers' gardens across the country.

GARDENBUILDINGS.COM
Go to gardenbuildings.com/directory/ for sources near you for all the garden structures covered in this book. Gardenbuildings.com is a database for locating companies that make, sell and deliver garden and leisure buildings, garden sheds, summerhouses, playhouses, pool houses and more. Or you can go to individual sites that I have suggested.

ARBORS

AUER-JORDAN
P.O. Box 1336
Healdsburg, CA 95448
707-838-1918
auerjordan.com

GARDEN ARCHES
1331 Meador Avenue, Ste. 105
Bellingham, WA 98229
800-947-7697
360-650-1587
gardenarches.com

WALPOLE WOODWORKERS
Fencing, arbors, pergolas and more
767 East Street
Walpole, MA 02081
800-343-6948
508-668-2800
walpolewoodworkers.com

BRIDGES

AVALON GARDEN BRIDGES
800-838-9085
avalongarden.com

GARDEN BRIDGES
800-518-7895
egardenbridges.com

GARDEN BRIDGES
P.O. Box 32
LeMarque, TX 77568
866-690-9273
gardenbridges.com

REDWOOD GARDEN BRIDGES
9196 East Shaw
Clovis, CA 93611
559-325-2597
redwoodgardenbridges.com

FENCING

BAMBOO & RATTAN WORKS, INC.
470 Oberlin Avenue South
Lakewood, NJ 08701
732-370-0220
bamboorattan.com

BOSTON TURNING WORKS
Finials for Gates and Fence Posts
120 Elm Street
Watertown, MA 02472
617-924-4747
bostonturningworks.com

OBELISKS

EXTERIOR ACCENTS
7140 Weddington Road, Suite 132
Concord, NC 28027
exterior-accents.com

PERGOLAS

BALDWIN PERGOLAS
180 Johnson Street
Middletown, CT 06457
800-344-5103
baldwinpergolas.com

RUSTIC GARDEN STRUCTURES
Box 374
Bynum, NC 27228
919-815-0215
rusticgardenstructures.com

PLAYHOUSES

SPIRIT ELEMENTS
Playhouses, pergolas, arbors, sheds,
gazeboes, trellises, cabin kits—you
name it, they've got it
6672 Gunpark Drive, #200
Boulder, CO 80301
800-511-1440
spiritelements.com

AMISH.NET
15802 Springdale Street, #14
Hunington Beach, CA 92649
714-846-0437
amishnet.com

SHEDS

CEDARSHED
DIY kits for gazeboes, sheds, etc.
800-830-8033
cedarshed.com

CUPOLAS AND WEATHERVANES
Cape Cod Cupola Co., Inc.
78 State Road
508-994-2119
North Dartmouth, MA 02747
capecodcupola.com

GARDEN SHED CATALOG
DIY blueprints
866-525-6789
gardenshedcatalogue.com

JAMAICA COTTAGE SHOP
Box 106
Jamaica, VT 05343
866-297-3760
jamaicacottageshop.com

GARDENSHEDS
651 Millcross Road
Lancaster, PA 17601
717-397-5430
gardensheds.com

HOMEPLACE STRUCTURES
866-768-8465
877-768-0804
homeplacestructures.com

SUMMERWOOD SHEDS AND GAZEBOES
735 Progress Avenue
Toronto, ON M1H 2W7
866-519-4634
summerwood.com

TRELLISES

GARDEN EXPRESSIONS
22627 SR 530 NE
Arlington, WA 98223
888-405-5234
gardenexpressions.com

TRELLIS STRUCTURES
888-285-4624
trellisstructures.com

WOOD CLASSICS
47 Steve's Lane
Gardiner, NY 12525
800-385-0030
woodclassics.com

YARDIAC
50A Littlejohn Glen Court
Greenville, SC 29615
866-927-3422
yardiac.com

UK AND EUROPEAN WEB
ADDRESSES FOR DESIGN IDEAS

BRIDGESFORGARDENS.COM

CEDARSHED.CO.UK

COULSONSBRIDGES.CO.UK

DOVECOTES.CO.UK

EGCC.BIZ (ENGLISH GARDEN CARPENTRY
COMPANY)

HERITAGEBUILDINGS.BE

HSPGARDENBUILDINGS.COM

NORTONGARDENSTRUCTURES.CO.UK

OAKLEAFGATES.CO.UK

PLAY-HOUSES.COM

SANCTUARY-SUMMERHOUSES.COM

STANFAIRBROTHER.CO.UK

Photo Credits

Richard Brown: 4.2, 5.3, page 3, 6A, 6.4, 6.6, 6.7, 10.6
Karen Bussolini: 4.5, 5.5, 5.6, 6.B, 7.7, 7A, 7C, 9.3, 9.4
Robin Cushman: 1.1, 3.1, 4.3, 4.4, 4B, 6.1, 7.1, 7.5, 8A, 9.1, 10.2
Ken Druse: 3.4, 3.7, 3A, 3B, 4A, 6C
Derek Fell: 2.1, 3.5 (above right), 3.6, 4.6, 5B, 6.2, 10.4
Susan and Dick Granville: 11.1–11.10
Harry Haralambou: 5A
Jerry Harpur: 1.2, 2.4, 3E, 5.1, 6.3, 7.2, 7.3, 8.7, 8.8, 8B, 9.2
Gordon Hayward: 2.2, 4.1, 5.4, 7B, 8.1, 10.1
Irene Jeruss: 1.3, 1.4, 5.2, 10.6
Dency Kane: 8.4
Carole Ottesen: 2.3, 3.3, 3C, 7.6, 8.2, 10.3, 10.7
Jerry Pavia: 3.2, 3D, 4C, 5B, 7.4, 8.3, 8.5, 8.6, 9.5

BOOKS BY ILLUSTRATOR PETER JOEL HARRISON

Peter Joel Harrison has written four studies on Historic American landscape detail that are published by John Wiley and Son. These hardcover volumes contain more than 1,100 images fashioned after copperplate engravings, all printed on cream paper using period typefaces and with marbleized end papers. They are the result of three decades of field research as Mr. Harrison traveled the country. Anyone involved in design, restoration or reproduction of historically accurate or historically inspired garden structures will find these books invaluable. His titles, all of which have the subtitle "*Authentic Details for Design and Restoration*," include:

Gazeboes and Trellises (ISBN 0-471-32198-2)
Fences (ISBN 0-471-32199-0)
Brick Pavement and Fence-Walls (ISBN 0-471-38337-6)
Garden Houses and Privies (ISBN 0-471-20332-7)
Bridges (coming soon)

To order:
877-762-2974
Fax: 800-605-2665

Peter Joel Harrison has also created a series of building plans available from Colonial Williamsburg, Williamsburg, Virginia. These unique draughts are patterned after the works of eighteenth-century artisans. The plates are modeled after period engravings. These will be of interest to architects, builders, landscapers and designers. Each 8 x 11-inch envelope contains three variations of the original subject. Not finding authentic plans for small buildings, Harrison conceived his own plans. *Historic Building Plans: The Architects and Builders Companion* includes the following subtitles:
Smokehouses
Wood Sheds
Privies
Wells
Fences: Series I–VII

To order:
The Book Sellers of Colonial Williamsburg
P.O. Box 1776
Williamsburg, VA 23187
757-565-8450
Fax: 757-565-8965

DESIGNS FOR FENCE PALES

Stratford Hall
Stratford, VA

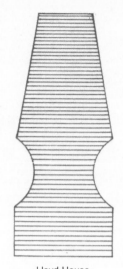

Lloyd House
Alexandria, VA

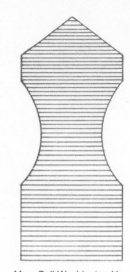

Mary Ball Washington House
Fredericksburg, VA

Mary Ball Washington House
Fredericksburg, VA

Cupola House
Edenton, NC

Newport, RI

Chestertown, MD

Cape May, NJ

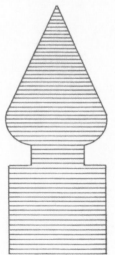

Shaker Village
Canterbury, NH

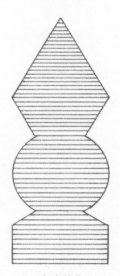

Arch Hall
Alexandria, VA

Colonial Williamsburg
Williamsburg, VA

Mount Vernon
Mount Vernon, VA